WRITING VIVID DIALOGUE

by Rayne Hall

WRITING VIVID DIALOGUE

Copyright Rayne Hall © 2015

(April 2016 Edition)

All Rights Reserved

Cover art and design by Erica Syverson

Interior illustrations by Hanna-Riikka

All rights reserved. Do not reproduce the content in whole or in part without the author's written permission.

CONTENTS

INTRODUCTION 5
1. A QUICK FIX TO ADD INSTANT INTEREST: ASK QUESTIONS 7
2. BUILD TENSION BY WITHHOLDING ANSWERS 9
3. GIVE EACH CHARACTER AN AGENDA
TO MAKE THE DIALOGUE VIBRANT 16
4. SHORT SENTENCES FOR NATURAL-SOUNDING DIALOGUE 19
5. HOW TO MAKE DIALOGUE PITHY, SIZZLING AND TIGHT 22
6. HOW TO GIVE EACH CHARACTER A UNIQUE VOICE 27
7. DIALOGUE TAGS—WHEN, WHERE,
HOW AND HOW OFTEN TO USE THEM 33
8. HOW TO AVOID NEEDLESS TAGS:
WHAT DOES THE SPEAKER DO? 38
9. HOW TO FORMAT DIALOGUE 41
10. A CURE FOR 'TALKING HEADS IN WHITE SPACE' 43
11. HOW DO MEN AND WOMEN TALK DIFFERENTLY? 45
12. HOW TO MAKE CHARACTERS APPEAR INTELLIGENT 51
13. DIALOGUE FOR MULTIPLE CHARACTERS 53
14. WHEN AND HOW TO USE BODY LANGUAGE 57
15. TELLING LIES 64
16. STARTING A STORY WITH DIALOGUE 67
17. INFORMING WITHOUT INFO-DUMPING 71
18. INTERNAL DIALOGUE: THINKING, NOT TALKING 74
19. INSULTS AND PROFANITY 77
20. FOREIGN LANGUAGES, ACCENTS AND JARGON 82
21. PARANORMAL AND TELEPATHIC COMMUNICATIONS 89

22. HOW CHILDREN AND TEENAGERS TALK 91

23. HOW PEOPLE TALK IN HISTORICAL FICTION 96

24. LEADERS AND FOLLOWERS, BOSSES AND MINIONS, RIVAL ALPHAS 102

25. ARGUMENTS 109

26. FLIRTATIOUS BANTER 111

27. CREATE DRAMATIC IMPACT WITH THREESOMES AND BACK-LOADING 116

DEAR READER 119

ACKNOWLEDGEMENTS 120

INTRODUCTION

Do you want to write fast-paced, exciting, sizzling dialogue?

This book reveals professional dialogue technique to characterise the speaker, carry the plot forward and entertain your readers.

This is not a beginner's guide. I assume that you have mastered the basics of fiction writing, and don't need an explanation of what dialogue is and why it matters for your story. But your dialogue isn't yet as strong as your story deserves. Perhaps it drags, perhaps the characters all sound the same, and perhaps it lacks tension, wit or sparkle.

I'll offer you a toolbox filled with techniques. These are not 'rules' every writer must follow, but tricks you can try. Pick, mix and match them to suit your characters and your story.

Some of these tools work for all kinds of dialogue, others solve specific problems—how to create male and female voices, how to present foreign languages and accents, how to present historical dialogue and flirtatious banter, how to write dialogue for alpha characters, for children and for liars.

I suggest you read once through the whole book to discover the tools in this kit, then return to the specific chapters which address the challenges of your current project.

You can apply the techniques to write new dialogue scenes, or to revise sections you've already written. When revising, you may want to compare the 'before' and 'after' versions. You'll be amazed how your dialogue scenes come to life.

I won't weigh this book down with literary theory. Sometimes I'll use examples—mostly from my own books, for copyright reasons—but in essence, this is about **your** writing, **your** stories, **your** dialogue.

If you like you can use this book as an advanced dialogue writing course, working your way through each chapter, doing the exercises in the chapter and the assignments at the end of each chapter. Or you can simply read the whole book to get a feel for what's in it, then choose the techniques you want to study and apply for the chapter you want to write or revise.

When referring to readers and characters, I'll sometimes use 'she' and sometimes 'he', simply to avoid the clunky 'he or she' constructions. The only time when gender matters in this book is when I compare female and male speech patterns, for example in Chapter 11. I'm using British English. If you're used to American, some of my word choices may look unfamiliar, and the syntax, grammar, punctuation and spelling varies as well, but the principles are the same.

Now open your manuscript. Let's improve your dialogue.

Rayne

1. A QUICK FIX TO ADD INSTANT INTEREST: ASK QUESTIONS

Have you written a dialogue scene that's basically okay, but needs to be more interesting?

I have a quick technique to enhance it without major changes. Questions rouse the reader's interest, so simply turn some statements into questions.

Here are some statements, and how you might phrase them as questions instead. You can see how much more intriguing the questions are.

"I want Santa to bring me a doll."
"Will Santa bring me a doll?"

"I'm looking for my wallet."
"Have you seen my wallet?"

"You haven't gone to church for a long time."
"When was the last time you went to church?"

"The dam may not hold much longer."
"How much longer will the dam hold?"

"You never seem to listen to what I say."

"Do you ever listen to what I say?"

"Maybe there really is a monster in the lake."

"What if there really is a monster in the lake?"

Suddenly, the speaker's words have undercurrents which add depth and engage the reader. If you like, you can apply this technique liberally, and pepper your dialogue scene with questions. Keep only a few statements so the rhythm doesn't get monotonous.

In the next chapter, I'll show you how to escalate this method to create tension.

ASSIGNMENT

Take a dialogue scene you've drafted and are not entirely happy with. Change several statements to questions. Enjoy the 'before-and-after' transformation.

2. BUILD TENSION BY WITHHOLDING ANSWERS

In this chapter, I'll show you an effective technique for making your dialogue simmer with tension.

One character (let's call her Mary) asks a question, and the other (John) doesn't answer. Now the reader definitely wants to know the answer, and also why John withholds it.

Perhaps Mary repeats the question. Does John answer now, or use a different avoidance tactic? With each unanswered question, the tension mounts. Why does John not reply? What does he have to hide? Why does Mary insist on drawing the information out of him? What does she suspect? Why does he resist? Which of the two will prevail?

Here are several ways you can handle this:

- Mary asks a question. John busies himself with some activity before replying. The reader senses that John needs time to compose his answer. Does he have to sort out his thoughts first, or perhaps he needs to compose himself and gather his courage, or maybe he is inventing a lie?

- Mary asks a question. John replies, but he doesn't answer the actual question. The reader senses that John has an unpalatable truth to hide but doesn't want to tell a lie. What John says may or may not hold a hint of what the problem is. Perhaps he's preparing the ground for a painful truth to be revealed later.

  Here's an example, provided by author Alice Gaines:

  "Daddy, will Santa bring me a bicycle this year?"
  "You know, honey, Santa can't always bring you exactly what you want. He has a lot of children to take care of, and sometimes he gets the orders mixed up."

Writing Vivid Dialogue

- Mary asks a question. John gives a perfunctory reply or no reply at all, and changes the subject. The reader knows that Mary has touched a sore spot and that John has a reason not to tell the truth.

- Mary asks a question. Instead of answering, John asks a question. This is my favourite technique because it hints at defensiveness and secrets. If you like, you can have the characters ping-pong questions at each other, escalating the tension with each exchange.

> Where were you between 9 and 10 pm last night?
>
> Why do you ask, officer?

Here are two examples:

Example 1: Wife and Husband

W: "Do you still love me?"
H: "Why are you asking?"
W: "Do you still truly love me?"
H: "Are you suddenly doubting my love?"
W: "Why won't you tell me that you still love me?"
H: "Do we have to talk about this now?"
W: "Why aren't you answering my question?"
H: "What do you want me to say?"

Example 2: Police Officer and Suspect

P: "Where were you between ten and eleven last night?"
S: "Why do you want to know?"
P: "Where were you between ten and eleven last night?"
S: "Where should I have been?"
P: "Why don't you tell me where you were?"
S: "Are you accusing me of something?"
P: "Do you have something to hide?"
S: "What makes you think I have something to hide?"

- Mary asks a question. John answers it eventually, but several chapters later. By now the reader senses a big secret, especially if Mary keeps probing and gets nowhere. When the answer finally comes, the truth may be as shocking for the reader as it is for Mary.

Writing Vivid Dialogue

SAMPLE DIALOGUE SCENE FROM *STORM DANCER*

This scene shows how I used answer avoidance (with many questions answered with questions) in one of my novels, *Storm Dancer*.

Background: Dahoud is a former siege commander who once ordered and committed atrocities. Leaving his dark past behind, he has assumed a new identity as a peace-loving, benevolent ruler. Nobody knows that he is the monster who ravaged the land. If his secret is found out, Dahoud's life will be forfeit and the country will erupt in war.

In this context, the reader already knows Dahoud's dark past. The tension arises from wondering what Sirria knows, and how Dahoud can protect his secret. Don't worry if you don't understand all that's going on – it's in the middle of a novel after all. Simply watch how Sirria keeps asking, and how Dahoud tries different methods of evasion.

Sirria hooked her arm around his. "Now, Dahoud, do you need a little pre-wedding chat with a crone?"

"Do you mean to tell me about the stallion and the mare? Not necessary." *He freed himself from her grasp and strode faster.*

"Where are your manners?" *she called.* "When a crone speaks, you stay and listen."

He turned and bowed.

"And you answer her questions." *Sirria stabbed a henna-stained finger at him.* "Does your bride know what kind of man she's about to wed? Does she know you were in the legions?"

He looked down the road, at the wooden balconies, at the honeysuckle smothering the mudbrick walls. "What makes you think I was in the legions?"

"What makes you think I was always a nomad?" *Sirria leant against the wall.* "Imagine me eight years younger, in the gown of a Zigazian matron, instead of this." She pulled at the side of her tunic. "Eight years ago, Dahoud. Eight years. Do you remember Ain Ziggur?"

Ain Ziggur. A city he had besieged under Paniour's command, before he had become a general, before he had campaigned in Koskara, before he had started wearing the intimidating mask. He had not expected anyone from those days to cross his path here.

At Ain Ziggur, the djinn had been in charge. Recall squeezed a fist around his throat. The siege. The women. His orders.

While the conquerors beheaded the surviving men, women barricaded themselves into the main temple and refused to come out. Centurion Dahoud had broken the door, and the women's resistance. He had ordered every woman raped.

He would have eaten the dust at Sirria's bare feet if he could undo the past. Nobody must know what kind of man he had been.

The rising sun glared on the town. Already, the air started to cook. The dry air burnt the back of Dahoud's throat.

"Because I remember, Dahoud." Sirria's voice was as sharp and unforgiving as an executioner's sword. "I remember every day the Quislaki legion besieged us, starved us, abused us. I remember our chief tormentor standing in the charred ruins of my home, with the bodies of my husband and my son at his feet. A man named Dahoud."

"Dahoud is a common name. Why do you think there's a connection?"

"Do you think the women of Zigazia would forget that name? Do you think we would forget what you ordered, and what you did? Do you think we would forget your face? You did not wear your famous mask then."

"I'm sorry, Sirria. More sorry than I can say." The words sounded inadequate even to his own ears. "I've changed. I'm not the man I was eight years ago. Can you believe me?"

A string of camels padded softly through the lane, laden with bales.

Sirria waited until they had passed. "I survived, fled to Koskara, became a herder. Then war came to Koskara, too, and with it came evil in the shape of a Quislaki commander, a man without scruples or conscience. A man so ruthless that some said he was possessed by a djinn. A man whose whispered name was enough to make women cower in fear. The Black Besieger." Her eyes pierced him like dagger points. "Did you know that when the Black Besieger died, the women in Koskara lit lamps of joy at every altar?"

It was bad enough if the Koskarans found out about his legion past. If anyone connected him with the Black Besieger, he would have no chance. Far from accepting his rule, they would roast him alive, and if he died, there would be more slaughter in Koskara, more war, more suffering.

He tried a different evasion. "You're happy now as a nomad, aren't you, Sirria?"

Her eyes darkened like thunderclouds. "Does the Black Besieger live? Was his funeral pyre faked?"

Below the tribal tattoo, her left cheek was mutilated, as if someone had slashed it with an angry knife.

"How did you come to Koskara, Sirria?" His palms sweated.

She adjusted her crimson shawl, covering the scar, without taking her eyes off him. "How did you come to Koskara again, Dahoud? How did you dare to?"

Dahoud's stomach knotted so tightly he could feel the pain. He dropped the useless shield of denial and faced his attacker. "I'm sorry for Ain Ziggur, and I'm sorry for every other citadel. I'm sorry for every death and every suffering, but it was in the past, Sirria. I've changed as much as you."

"Doesn't your bride have the right to know she's wedding a beast? Doesn't every woman in Koskara need to know that a monster rules the land?" She stepped so close to him that he could feel her searing breath on his throat. "Why shouldn't I scream the truth from the *roof? Why shouldn't I tell Mansour? Why shouldn't I expose you as the impostor you are?"*

Dahoud's mouth was drier than desert sand. "What's the price for your silence?"

"When the time comes, I'll let you know." She laughed softly and pointed at a curtain of clay-bead strings. "Here's the bathhouse. Enjoy the experience. Have a water-filled day, my Lord, and a pleasant wedding night."

She floated away in a swish of coloured shawls.

ASSIGNMENT

Is there a situation in your current work in progress where one character probes and the other evades? If not, could you insert one? Write (or rewrite) it, using one or several of the suggested techniques.

Read it aloud. Can you feel the simmering tension? Then you've nailed it.

3. GIVE EACH CHARACTER AN AGENDA TO MAKE THE DIALOGUE VIBRANT

Your dialogue scene becomes vibrant if every character has an agenda. Yes, every character—even the walk-on parts.

In real life, people talk a lot without purpose, just out of boredom or to meet social obligations. Fiction dialogue is different.

Some characters are open about their agenda, stating outright what they want. Others are subtle, manipulative or shy.

Let's say six people are having dinner at Poshaughty Manor: Lady Mary, Lord John, their adult son Henry and twelve-year-old daughter Henriette, as well Henriette's governess and Henry's new girlfriend Suzie. A footman serves.

Here are some ideas for hidden agendas, never openly admitted:

- Lady Mary wants to expose and draw attention to Suzie's ignorance and clumsiness, so Henry won't think of marrying her.

- Suzie wants to make her potential future mother-in-law, Lady Mary like her.

- Sir John wants this dinner to be over with, so he can return to the peace and quiet of his study.

- Henry wants to keep the conversation away from cards, casinos and the unfortunate matter of his gambling debts of which Suzie must never learn.

- Henriette, lonely and bored at Poshaughty Manor, wants her brother Henry to spend more time with her.

- The footman wants to impress with his skill, to get the butler position which will soon fall vacant.

- The governess wants to find out which nights Lady Mary and Sir John will be absent from Poshaughty Manor, she can inform her accomplice, the jewel thief.

The reader probably knows what the Point of View character wants, but not necessarily what the others are after. She may learn about some of them later, for example about the governess's complicity in the jewel thefts, but others are not part of the story and don't matter to the plot, such as the footman's ambitions. Yet even the irrelevant agendas add vibrancy to the scene.

Try it for yourself with this exercise: let's say John and Mary are young people on a first date in a restaurant. The plot of the scene is about John and Mary. Other characters have walk-on parts, such as the waiter who serves them.

John asks the waiter what wine he recommends. This brief exchange simply serves to inject variety, so the whole scene isn't constant John-and-Mary banter. It's of little relevance to the plot, and the waiter will never play a role again.

Go ahead, write those two lines.

John: "xxx"

Waiter: "xxxx"

Done? Good job. You've probably come up with an appropriate exchange, but not spent much thought on crafting it because the waiter is unimportant.

Now give both John and the waiter an agenda.

Let's say, John wants to impress his date, and wants to hide his ignorance of wines.

The waiter's agenda is to get a big tip.

Write this. I bet it is immediately more interesting.

If you like, play with the following variations. Pick one agenda for John, and one for the waiter.

Writing Vivid Dialogue

Possible agendas for John:

- John tries to engage the waiter in conversation, so he can avoid the topic Mary wants to talk about.
- John aims to emphasise his wealth and generosity.
- John seeks to get rid of the waiter, so he can continue his intimate conversation with Mary.
- John wants to distract the waiter's attention from something embarrassing Mary is doing.

Possible agendas for the waiter:

- The waiter is a foreign student who seeks to practise his English.
- The waiter is an aspiring actor. He hopes to gain the attention of the casting director at the next table.
- The waiter is stressed, and he wants to finish this table quickly.
- The waiter earns a bonus each time a patron orders the most expensive wine. He tries to persuade John to order this wine.

Have fun!

ASSIGNMENT

Choose a scene from a fiction draft you've written, where the dialogue feels dull. Revise it so each character has an agenda.

Or

Write a new scene and give each character an agenda to pursue.

4. SHORT SENTENCES FOR NATURAL-SOUNDING DIALOGUE

Dialogue needs to sound real—but the way people talk in real life doesn't sound right in fiction. As an author, aim not to recreate real conversations, but to create an illusion of reality.

If you imitate real life dialogue too closely, you'll end up with unfocussed, dragging drivel. Instead, I suggest a technique which is exactly the opposite of how real people talk.

Write the dialogue in short sentences—shorter than the narrative sentences, and much shorter than the rambling run-ons you hear in real life. The shorter the sentences, the more 'real' they feel to the reader.

Simply take any dialogue sentence that's longer than twelve words and split it into two or more short ones, perhaps shaving off unneeded words at the same time. Here are two examples.

Before

"I admit haven't been the best husband, but I promised to love you, for better or for worse, and I meant it and still do.""

After

"I' admit I haven't been the best husband. But I promised to love you, for better or for worse. I meant it. I still do.""

Before

"Does that look on your face mean you expected not me, but someone else, such as that Italian who lives in the next door flat?"

After

"You look surprised. Did you expect someone else? That Italian from next door?""

Here is another technique for real-sounding dialogue:

Use contractions (*hasn't, haven't, hadn't, doesn't, don't, didn't, won't, wouldn't, shan't, shouldn't, I'm, I've, you're* and so on). They give the dialogue a natural flavour.

Before

"You are a fool. You should not have done that.""

After

"You're a fool. You shouldn't have done that."

However, you can leave off the contractions when characters speak in a formal context or seek to emphasise something: " *"You are my daughter, and I am telling you: You shall not see this man again."*

Foreigners grappling with the English language may also not use contractions.

Another factor to bear in mind for realistic dialogue is not to have the characters address one another by name all the time:

Before

"Have you seen my purse, John?"
"Nope, Mary, I haven't.
"But, John, you were here all the time."
"Sorry, Mary, I have no idea what you're talking about."

After

"Have you seen my purse?"
"Nope, I haven't."
"But you were here all the time."
"Sorry, I have no idea what you're talking about."

The exception is when one character tries to get the other's attention:

"John!" Mary raced across the road. "Wait for me, John!"

ASSIGNMENT

Take a dialogue scene you've drafted. Do the characters talk in long sentences? (I don't want to lay down the rule for what constitutes 'long' but as a guideline, I suggest anything longer than twelve words.) If yes, see if you can split those long sentences into several short ones. At the same time, use contractions if appropriate.

Does it sound more natural now? It should.

5. HOW TO MAKE DIALOGUE PITHY, SIZZLING AND TIGHT

Dialogue scenes penned by inexperienced writers tend to drag. Even seasoned writers struggle to keep the verbal exchanges pithy.

Here are some techniques. The main point is to stop imitating real life chats. Converted into print, real conversations are tediously slow-paced and dull.

LEAVE OUT THE BORING BITS

Ruthlessly cut anything that doesn't drive the plot forward. Where real people use several to-and-fro exchanges, condense it to just one. The best candidates for cutting are greetings, courtesies, and ritualised small talk. In real life, they're polite and often crucial. In fiction, they're tedious ballast that puts readers off.

Here's an example of a real life exchange:

"Hi, John."
"Hi, Mary."
"How have you been, John?"
"Fine, thanks, and you?"
"Not too bad. What are you doing this weekend, any plans?"
"Oh, this and that. Not sure yet. How about you?"
"I may go to the beach concert. Are you going?"
"Dunno yet. Why do you ask? Perhaps."

How do you feel reading this? I bet you're bored, and if you saw this in a novel, you'd skip some paragraphs in search of more exciting stuff.

Now compare this version:

"Hi John. Will you go to the beach concert?"
"Why do you ask?"

This is much tighter and more exciting, with the beginnings of sizzling tensions. The reader is hooked. She wants to know: will John go to the concert? What interest does Mary have in whether or not he goes? Why does he evade? What's going on between those two, and what's going to happen?

DON'T REPEAT

When people talk in real life, they often say the same thing over and over until it sinks in, but in fiction dialogue, tight speech without repetition creates more emphasis.

Say everything just once, in the snappiest way possible, and the reader pays attention. If you repeat content, the reader tunes out.

LEAVE OUT UNNECESSARY WORDS

The fewer words, the snappier the dialogue.

In real life, people often talk faster than they think, so they use filler words like 'really' and 'quite' to give their brain time to catch up with the mouth.

When people converse in tight phrases, the dialogue sizzles. This works especially well for hero/heroine dialogues, and for anything involving the villain.

Cut all superfluous words from your characters' speeches. Play around with what they say until it's as tight as you can make it.

Superfluous words may be, for example: q*uite, rather, so to speak, in a way, therefore, really, very, completely, totally, absolutely, for the purpose of, somewhat, somehow, anyway.*

Cutting a few words and phrases can make dialogue more realistic and more exciting. But don't get carried away. Keep some unnecessary words if they serve to characterise the speaker.

Here are examples of 'wordy' and 'tight' dialogue:

Wordy:

"I'm not sure I understand what you're saying, Mary. Let me get this right. Are you saying that you're leaving me?"

Tight:

"You're leaving me?"

Wordy:

"You know, I reckon you may be missing a chance that won't come again in this lifetime. Are you absolutely sure you want to do that?"

Tight:

"Do you want to miss this chance?"

Wordy:

"At least tell me where you're going."

"It's really obvious where I'm going, after what has just happened. I'm going home, of course. You shouldn't need to ask."

Tight:

"Where are you going?"

"Home."

Wordy:

"What John told you just now isn't true. It was really a lie."

Tight:

"John lied."

Tightening Exercise:

Since it's easier to tighten other people's writing, you may want to practise with these lines before you edit your own:

1. "I can't say I'm completely sure about this."
2. "I'm sorry but I guess that's it, then, really."
3. "This is simply so unbelievable."
4. "I must say, the time has come when it has become absolutely necessary that all of us unite for our cause."
5. "You may not like me asking this, but I have to know, so please tell me the truth why you are late."

CREATE ZINGERS

Zingers are pithy, succinct, evocative one-liners. In just a few words, the character expresses a whole world of meaning and attitude.

In real life, people don't talk in zingers. They simply don't have time to refine every uttering until it's diamond-sharp. If you want to hear zingers, watch a movie. Scriptwriters have refined them to an art.

Readers love zingers—but how do you create them?

Pick an existing dialogue line in which an important character says something impactful or provocative. Prune it. Shave off every word that's not absolutely necessary, until you're left with the bare essence. Replace dull words with short vivid ones. Now it zings.

Example (without Zinger):

Mary: "You don't know what kind of man my husband is, and what he's capable of."

John: *"I'm starting to think maybe you don't know your husband all that well yourself."*

The same with Zinger:

Mary: *"You don't know what kind of man my husband is, and what he's capable of."*

John: *"Do you?"*

Most zingers work only in the context of the story, so I can't give you many examples because you'd need to read the book to understand what they're about.

The character who delivers a zinger comes across as clever, spunky, witty, superior—perfect for your heroine and hero. Your villain may fling zingers, too. Perhaps one or two other important characters use them as well. But don't waste zingers on minor characters.

Zingers work especially well in confrontation scenes and for flirtatious banter. They also make brilliant parting shots. Whoever has the last word, wins – and if the last word happens to be a zinger, the effect is a big Wow!

ASSIGNMENT

Choose an important dialogue scene from a fiction draft, and revise it. Make it tight—edit out the unnecessary bits and the repetitions, and pare the words until it becomes snappy. Can you think of a zinger, or maybe several?

6. HOW TO GIVE EACH CHARACTER A UNIQUE VOICE

Do your characters all sound the same? Do they talk the way their author talks? In this section you'll learn how to make them sound differently.

Think of each character's key personality traits. Define them in adjectives, for example, honest, sensitive, ambitious, greedy, pessimistic, resentful. I suggest five for the main protagonist, four for main characters, three for minor characters and two for walk-on roles. (Of course your characters are more complex than a five-word description, but for this technique, it's best to focus on the key traits.)

Whenever the character speaks, her words reflect one of those traits, either in content (what she says) or in style (how she says it). Let the characters' personalities shine through in everything they say.

Here are some examples of how the content can reflect the personality.

Resentful: "Without Mary's meddling, we would have won the award."

Forgiving: "Mary wasn't up to the task, but she did her best."

Ambitious: "Let's go for next year's award and do better."

Pessimistic: "Is it worth trying again next year? We don't have a real chance."

Optimistic: "Is it worth trying again next year? We may stand a better chance then."

Cynical: "How much does it cost to bribe the judges? Does our budget stretch that far?"

How would a person with these characteristics talk? What word choices and speech patterns reflect this personality? Here are some examples:

Writing Vivid Dialogue

Self-centred: this person begins everything she says with 'I...' The words 'me', 'my', 'mine' also feature a lot in her conversation.

Timid, insecure: she uses qualifiers and excuses. Her conversations contain *"rather", "quite", "somewhat", "I would like to say", "maybe", "On the other hand", "If I may say so", "Forgive me for being so outspoken, but", "This may sound strange, but", "I think that perhaps", "more or less"*. She prefaces requests and statements with apologies: *"I'm sorry to bother you. I wonder if it's possible to..." "I'm probably wrong, but..."*

Pompous: a multi-syllabic word in every sentence: *"The exoneration of the thefts..." "We must take into consideration that..."*

Bossy: often phrases sentences as commands. *"Take a taxi." "Call me tomorrow."*

Status-seeking: name drops and mentions status symbols at every opportunity: *"Last week, the duchess told me..." "When I parked my Porsche..."*

Gushing: this character talks in superlatives like *"the cutest", "the worst", "the most terrifying"*, with additions of *"absolutely", "totally", "completely", "utterly", "ever", "never", "forever"*.

Let's look how this might work in practice. Four different people say, *"I'm late because there was an hour-long queue."*

Self-centred character: *"I'm sorry I'm late. I had to wait a precious hour in a queue, as if I didn't have more important things to do."*

Insecure, indecisive, weak character: *"I'm sorry I'm rather late. There was quite a queue, maybe an hour."*

Gushing, effusive, highly-strung character: *"I'm soooo sorry I'm late. The queue there was absolutely appalling, and I had to wait forever and ever."*

Bossy character: *"Don't think I'm late on purpose. Imagine standing in a queue for an hour."*

If these people talk about the day their house burnt down, they may phrase it like this:

Self-centred character: *"I tell you, I've never been so frightened in my life. This was my home, my shelter, my everything. I stood there watching my belongings go up in flames, and my memories with it. My husband was as helpless as I. I'm just glad my kids are safe."*

Insecure, indecisive, weak character: *"The fire was quite fierce, and spread rather quickly. We all got out more or less in time, but if I may say so, we were somewhat shaken."*

Gushing, effusive, highly-strung character: *"It was absolutely horrifying, the worst nightmare. There was this unbelievably tremendous heat, the hugest flames you've ever seen, and the biggest column of the darkest smoke. It went on forever and ever, and I lost absolutely everything. It was utterly devastating."*

Bossy character: *"Imagine the flames, the smoke, the heat. Don't think anyone could have saved anything. Never let your own kids play with matches."*

Here's an exercise for you to try:

Imagine the two scenarios where a character apologises for being late and where she talks about her house burnt down.

Think about how would one of these types talk?

- a pious optimist
- a resentful pessimist

Have fun!

ALSO CONSIDER

You may find the techniques in Chapters 11, 12, 22 and 24 useful too.

SAMPLE DIALOGUE FROM *STORM DANCER*

Here is another section from my dark epic fantasy novel *Storm Dancer*. Dahoud's bride has arrived for their wedding. This is to be an arranged marriage between willing partners. Dahoud is in love with Esha, but does not actually know her well. At this stage, the reader still roots with Dahoud for the success of this match.

Reading this excerpt, you probably won't understand the full context, but observe how Esha's dialogue give clues to Esha's personality: effusive, self-obsessed, insensitive, status-oriented, scheming. The reader will absorb these cues – some consciously, some subconsciously – and begin to wonder if Dahoud is making a mistake.

He cleared his throat. "Esha, you can't stay here."

Her eyes widened with alarm. "Don't you want me?"

He could smell her perfume, her hair, her skin. Her locks danced around the white skin of her neck, down over her tunic, over the swell of her breasts. "I'm glad you've accepted my proposal. Only... I didn't expect you so soon."

Esha smiled as if he had complimented her. "The camels and servants we borrowed from Lord Adil. He's a most amazingly generous man."

"He is." Dahoud remembered Tarkan's father from many years ago. "Perhaps you would like to stay with him for a while. I'm sure he'll enjoy your company."

"I've come to get married."

"Esha, there are a few things you need to be aware of," he said carefully. "Koskara is very hot at this time of the year, and there are some local problems with rebels."

"The locals will adore weddings, so we'll have the biggest celebration they've seen for ages, four days long, with lots of food and entertainment. I'll do absolutely anything that's necessary."

A traditional wedding might indeed make them popular. "Anything? Would you be willing, for example, to live in a yurt?"

"A yurt? You mean living a tent?" For a moment, her face stiffened as if she had seen a poisonous spider on her spoon. Then it relaxed, and her eyes narrowed like those of an officer assessing battle plans. "That's a fabulous strategy for getting popular with the natives, and I'm not in the least afraid of discomfort."

She ate little, lifting her spoon daintily with small white hands. She talked about how peacock fans were fashionable at court this season, how tiring the journey had been in the summer heat, and how annoying she found the presence of poultry.

Dahoud drank her beauty as thirstily as a camel sucking up water. Her skin was creamy-white like a lamb's fleece, her hips curved like a succulent fig, and her breasts plump like a pair of cushions to sink his head into.

He had to tell her the truth about himself, but the words stuck in his throat.

"Are you sure you want to wed me?" he managed at last.

"Absolutely, and I'm ever so grateful you asked for me. It was simply the only way for me to escape my horrid betrothal."

"Betrothal?" he repeated.

"To my father's former chief councillor. He seemed destined to become a Lord, but grew addicted to smoking joy-flowers until his mind was utterly befuddled. It was disgusting. When my father sacked him, this failure of a man couldn't find work elsewhere. If I had to marry that revolting wreck, my daughters would be commoners. I kept petitioning the Consort most fervently to release me from this abominable betrothal. Finally, he let me choose between that appalling feeblehead and a ready-made Lord, which is the most wonderful opportunity." Her cheeks tinged with a becoming blush. "I can speak freely of it now, can't I? I really think I'm amazingly fond of you."

His heart was aflutter like a bird, ready to soar. A woman liked him. But she did not know the truth yet.

"We need not marry at once. We can delay until you're used to me, and to Koskara."

"Dahoud, I'm fully aware that Koskara is a dreadfully backward province. I've travelled here to marry you and beget a child. I want to start without delay." *Her lash-veiled grey gaze sent hot blushes into his cheeks.*

"There's something you need to know. Nobody else in Koskara does." *Cold sweat ran down his temples.* "I was a soldier once."

"Oh." *For a moment, her mouth drooped, but her face quickly recovered its radiance.* "It doesn't matter. You're a lord-satrap now. I won't hold your lowly origins against you, or disclose them to anyone."

ASSIGNMENT

Take a dialogue scene you've drafted or want to write. Identify between two and five core personality traits for each speaker. Write, rewrite or tweak everything the characters say so it reflects at least one of their traits.

7. DIALOGUE TAGS—WHEN, WHERE, HOW AND HOW OFTEN TO USE THEM

To make it easier for the reader to understand who says what, writers add tags: 'he said', 'she asked', 'I grumbled'.

A tag usually comes at the end, after the spoken sentence. This works great if the character says just a few words. For example:

"Give me that book," Mary said.

It can also come in the middle, which is effective when the character speaks two or more sentences.

"No, it's mine," John said. "Leave me alone, or I'll call the police."

Sometimes it can come at the beginning, although this can give your prose an old-fashioned, clunky feel:

Mary said: "Give me that book."

WHEN ARE TAGS NEEDED?

Tags are not necessary every time a character opens his mouth. If it's clear who's talking, you can skip the tag. Let's say John and Mary are having an argument. Then *"You're the vilest man I've ever met"* doesn't need a tag to indicate that it's Mary who says this.

You may have read 'rules for writers' decreeing that tags must always be used when a character says something, and others stating that dialogue should never be tagged, while yet others insist that every fourth line has to be tagged, or every fifth, or some other such ordinance.

Forget those demands. Let other writers follow what rules they wish to make for their own work, and decide for yourself what suits your story. I certainly won't set rules for you to obey.

Writing Vivid Dialogue

My advice is simple. Use as many tags as needed, and as few as possible.

Does the tag aid the scene's clarity? Use it. If it doesn't, cut. I'll give you some tips later in this chapter and the next.

'SAID' VERSUS OTHER TAGS

Another set of 'rules' concerns the word 'said'. Some insist that 'he/she/I said' is the only acceptable tag, while others demand that any other tag is acceptable but 'he/she/I said' must be avoided.

Ignore those rules, too.

If 'he/she/I said' works in your story, use it. If something else works better, use that. Pick a verb that shows how the person speaks: he/she muttered, shouted, asked, queried, growled, yelled, threatened, grumbled, demanded, asked, ordered, commanded, pleaded, begged, claimed, boasted, insisted, repeated, whined... This can be very effective.

"Give me that book," Mary demanded.
"Give me that book," Mary whispered.
"Give me that book," Mary shouted.
"Give me that book," Mary ordered.
"Give me that book," Mary begged.

But avoid complicated verbs such as he *interrogated* and *she expostulated*. Short, simple verbs are best.

Guard against over-using the word 'whisper' as a tag. It's not wrong, but many new writers use it so often that it has become a flag by which editors recognise the novice.

Another tag to be careful about is 'sigh'. Not only is this word overused by beginner writers, but it doesn't really work as a tag.

"All I have worked for in my life lies in ruin and ashes," she sighed.

It's not possible to sigh that sentence. Try it.

'Hiss' can work—but only for short bursts containing 's' sounds.

Correct: *"Stay silent!" she hissed.*
Wrong: *"Be quiet!" she hissed.*

ADVERBS—AVOID IF POSSIBLE

The next 'rule' you may have come across concerns adverbs—the words ending in '-ly' which explain the verb, such as angrily, quickly, cheerfully. Some people—including editors—insist that all adverbs are bad and must be eliminated. I wouldn't go that far, but I agree that they're best avoided, because they can make your writing appear stiff and clumsy.

What the character says and does is often clear enough not to need adverbs. Take this example:

'You bastard!" she said angrily, slamming the door.

The adverb 'angrily' can be deleted because it's clear that this character is angry.

(Actually, I'd also cut the tag 'she said', but we'll get to that later.)

Similarly, 'he screamed' doesn't need the adverb 'loudly', 'she snapped' doesn't need 'irritably' and 'he muttered' doesn't need 'quietly'.

Choose your verbs with care, and you'll rarely need adverbs to explain them.

You may want to practise with the following sentences. Replace the bland verb with a vivid one and cut the adverb:

"Help! Is anybody here?" Mary asked loudly.
"If you do this, I will kill you," John said threateningly.
"Can you do this?" John said questioningly.
"Give me that book," Mary said demandingly.

ACTIONS MAKE TAGS UNNECESSARY

When a character acts and speaks, the action is enough to attribute the dialogue, so you don't need a tag. By deleting the tag, you can make your writing tighter and more exciting.

Before:

John scratched his head and said, "I wonder if that's true."

After:

John scratched his head. "I wonder if that's true."

Before:

"You bastard!" Mary shouted and slammed the door.

After:

"You bastard!" Mary slammed the door.

Before:

"We're almost there," John said, squeezing Mary's hand. "I can see the door."

After:

"We're almost there." John squeezed Mary's hand. "I can see the door."

For practice, edit the following sentences:

"Just five more minutes," John said, panting with effort.
Mary clutched the book to her chest. "This is mine," she said.
"I know your secret," Mary said and giggled. "I've seen what you do on Thursday nights."

In the next chapter, we'll take a deeper look at how you can use action to attribute dialogue without tags.

ASSIGNMENT

Choose a dialogue scene you've written. Cut out any superfluous tags and adverbs. There's no 'right' or 'wrong' here. You decide what is needed for clarity and what can go. Are you satisfied with the new version? Then you've done it right.

8. HOW TO AVOID NEEDLESS TAGS: WHAT DOES THE SPEAKER DO?

Instead of tags, you can use beats—and in most cases, they're the better choice because they're vivid.

Dialogue beats are separate sentences about something the speaking character does. They imply, rather than tell, that this character speaks. (In different contexts, the word 'beat' may mean 'plot event'. Don't let this confuse you.)

A dialogue beat can be an action, or body language, or a facial expression, or a tone of voice. Beats can tell us a lot about a person and their mood and feelings. A beat can come before or after the spoken words, or in the middle.

Examples for beats with body language:

Mary stretched out her hand. "Give me that book, John."
"No, it's mine." *John clutched the book to his chest.* "Leave me alone."
Mary jumped up. "Give me that book at once!"
"No. Stupid bitch." *John stuck out his tongue.*

Examples for beats with facial expression:

Mary's eyes narrowed. "Give me that book, John."
John frowned. "No, it's mine. Leave me alone."
"Give me that book at once!" *Mary's eyes drilled into him.*
"No." *John's face reddened with anger.* "Stupid bitch!"

Examples for beats with tone of voice:

"No, it's mine. Leave me alone." John's voice boomed through the empty space.

"Give me that book at once." Mary's voice was a coarse whisper.

Examples for beats with action:

Mary counted five breaths to calm herself and keep her temper.
"Give me that book at once."
"No. Stupid bitch!" John rushed out of the room and slammed the door behind him.

HOW TO USE BEATS

Mix up different types of dialogue beats—action, body language and so on—in your dialogue scene.

Vary the placement as well, putting some beats before the speech, some after, and some in the middle. 'Putting it in the middle' doesn't mean exactly halfway through. A good place is after the first few words, perhaps after the first sentence.

When one character has a long speech, you can intersperse it with several beats.

When you use a beat, leave out the tag, because it's not necessary.

If you use a beat, the speech ends with a period, not a comma.

ALSO CONSIDER

The sections on body language and tone of voice in Chapter 14 and the advice how to avoid talking heads in white space in Chapter 10 provide further techniques.

ASSIGNMENT

Pick a dialogue scene you want to revise. Replace tags with beats where possible.

Or

Write a new dialogue scene without using any tags, using beats to show who's talking.

9. HOW TO FORMAT DIALOGUE

Formatting and punctuating dialogue can be confusing, with exceptions, exceptions to exceptions, and rules which differ not only between British and American English, but from publisher to publisher.

Ignore the complications. All you need are these three basics:

1. When a new person speaks, start a new paragraph.
2. What the person does goes in the same paragraph as what he says.

   Here's an example.

   "Where are you going?" Mary clasped his arm.
   John shrugged himself free. "None of your business."
   "But... but you promised..."
   "I don't have time for this." At the door, he paused. "I'm sorry, love."

3. Use a comma at the end of the speech only if a tag follows. Otherwise, use a full stop (American: a period.)

   Wrong:
   "I'm not sure about this," she scratched her head.

   Right:
   "I'm not sure about this." She scratched her head.

Keep these three rules in mind, and 99.9% of all eventualities will be covered and correct, and your writing will look professional. Whether the remaining 0.1% are correct depends on whom you ask, which school of punctuation they subscribe to and which publisher they work for.

If publishers want to buy your novel, they'll either show you the 'house style' they want you to follow, or fix those details the way they want them. Until then, don't worry.

ASSIGNMENT

Look over a dialogue scene you've written—especially if you're about to submit it to an agent or publisher, or if you plan to indie-publish it—and apply those three rules.

10. A CURE FOR 'TALKING HEADS IN WHITE SPACE'

When agents and editors reject your book, they may explain that it's because of 'talking heads dialogue' or dialogue 'in white space' ... or even 'talking heads in white space'.

What do they mean? And how do you fix this flaw?

'Talking heads' means pure dialogue. The characters don't do anything besides conversing. In fiction, this feels stilted and dull.

The solution is simple: give the characters something to do besides talking.

The obvious choice is to let them have a meal. Then you can use the motions of eating and drinking as beats.

"What do you think, John?" Mary passed him the potatoes. "Will Grandma sell the house?"

Meals work well, especially for dialogue involving several people, but take care not to do this too often. If all the conversations in your book happen while the characters eat and drink, it soon becomes tedious.

Give your characters something useful to do. It doesn't need to be exciting action—a mundane task can create a vivid contrast for gruesome dialogue.

"Aim at his kidneys, and twist the blade in the wound." Mary squirted lemon-scented soap into the basin. "Make it gory and painful."

Better still, put your characters to work at something plot-relevant, preferably with time running out. Perhaps they are repairing the wrecked boat to get off the prison island before their guards discover their absence. Maybe they build a hut to shelter them against the imminent monsoon, or try to get the party decorations up before the

Writing Vivid Dialogue

first guests arrive. Mix action and dialogue, and the 'talking heads' problem is gone.

'White space' refers to scenes which don't seem to have a clear location and could be taking place anywhere. "But this scene has a real setting," many novice writers protest. "I've described it in detail at the beginning of the scene."

That's exactly the problem. Inexperienced writers dump a lot of location description at the beginning of the scene, and then don't mention the setting again.

Here are two suggested solutions:

1. Take that chunk of setting description, split it into several small parts, and sprinkle those throughout the scene.
2. Create dialogue beats in which the characters interact with their environment, perhaps touching an item of furniture.

Mary tapped her talons on the desk. "Get to the point."

"So it's true. Tell me more." *Mary dropped into the dark leather chair. The upholstery squealed under her weight.*

Mary glanced at the ornate grandfather clock. "We have about ten minutes."

ASSIGNMENT

Revise a draft scene which suffers from 'talking heads' and/or 'white space'.

Or

Write a new dialogue scene for your novel. Place it in an unusual location and give your characters an important task to carry out while they talk.

11. HOW DO MEN AND WOMEN TALK DIFFERENTLY?

In real life, we can easily tell men's voices from women's, and you want to achieve the same in your fiction. Unfortunately, the main difference—most male voices are deeper—doesn't work in prose. So how can you make men sound different from women?

In this section, I'll show you some techniques. Please bear in mind that they don't apply to every man and every woman in every context and society. Only you can decide which suggestion is right for your characters and your story.

1. Women talk more than men.

On average, women communicate more often, and use more words than their male counterparts. Many scientific studies have been devoted to this, counting and comparing the number of words. Apparently, the difference is due to specific proteins in the brain. Unfortunately, the studies don't agree about results. While one study claims women speak 20,000 words per day compared with men's 7,000, another cites 18,000: 2,000. Yet others find that the ratio depends on the context, and in certain situations men actually talk more.

What does this mean for your fiction? You may want to give your female characters a more generous word allowance than the men. The precise ratio doesn't matter, and the difference doesn't have to be huge—perhaps two or three words every time they speak.

Of course, your characters may differ from the average population anyway. The heroine of your novel may be laconic while her boyfriend chatters all the time.

2. Women mention their emotions more often.

It's unclear whether this is due to biological differences in the brain, to evolutionary gender differentiation, to social conditioning or to all three, but on average, men talk about feelings less often than women.

This doesn't mean that men are hiding or suppressing their emotions. They simply prefer to express them through body language or action rather than words. In conversation, they see no reason why they should emphasise emotions if it's clear how they feel.

It doesn't mean that women are indiscriminately displaying emotions either. To them, frankness about feelings is a way to avoid misunderstandings and to build trust.

Let's look at a typical male versus female talk.

After a visit to the cinema, this is what a woman may say to her best friend, *"I'm so disappointed. The film was crap."*

A man talking to his buddy says, *"The film was crap."*

The message is the same, and the companions get the meaning. The women's version is a little longer, and her emotion is emphasised. The man's comment is brief, and it's clear what he feels but the emotion is not spelled out.

3. Men use dialogue to identify their place in the pecking order.

When two men meet for the first time, they'll seek and give clues about who ranks above whom. In the modern world, they often do this by casually mentioning their job title, or by asking the other guy, "What do you do?"

The exchange is amicable, and seldom fraught with rivalry and tension. Men don't normally begrudge another man's status, they simply feel more comfortable knowing. This feature is probably hard-wired into the male brain.

When two male characters in your fiction meet for the first time, include some kind of 'rank comparison' at the beginning of the conversation. It doesn't have to be much, just a few words.

If your story has two male characters who are rivals for the same award, job or woman, you can take this 'pecking order' habit further. Their dialogue will simmer with tension as each emphasises his own higher rank or tries to lower the other man's place in the hierarchy.

For more about this, see Chapter 24.

4. Men use more posture, women more facial expressions.

This is another surprising difference, apparently hardwired into the human psyche. Women can read facial expressions better, can recognise a far greater number of them, and use them a lot more.

Where the average man can tell whether a face looks happy or unhappy, a woman sees nuances.

Men, however, are aware of postures. They notice when someone shifts their posture and know what it means. Men can communicate with other men through posture alone—especially messages about their place in the pecking order and arguments over who is the dominant male in the room—while the women don't even notice that an exchange is going on.

How can you use this in your fiction? For dialogue between men, use posture beats, and for conversations between women, facial expressions.

John squared his shoulders. "What did you say?"

Mary's brows drew together. "What did you say?"

5. Women get to the point more slowly.

When men want to get a message across or to ask a favour, they'll ask directly:

"May I borrow your lawn mower?"

Women tend to approach the subject more slowly, circling around it and providing background information before they get to the point.

"May I ask you a favour? My mother-in-law is coming tomorrow, and we'll have tea in the garden. I haven't cut the grass for ages, because my lawn mower is broken. Could I possibly borrow yours?"

I have no idea whether this difference stems from brain proteins or is purely social conditioning, but I've observed it in cultures across the world.

6. Men don't compliment other men on their appearance.

While women habitually comment on other women's looks, hairstyles and apparel – as a matter of courtesy and interest – men rarely do this with other men. If a man praises another man's shirt, that would make the compliment's recipient feel uncomfortable. It can also be seen as a gay thing.

However, men compliment women on their looks often and easily. Women occasionally compliment men on their clothes choice or a new hairstyle.

7. Social and cultural norms

Depending on where your characters grew up and where they live now, they will have acquired additional male or female patterns which show in dialogue.

For example, in some regions women aren't supposed to let foul language pass their lips, but men use swearwords liberally. In some countries, it's considered rude for a man to contradict a woman, while in others, females won't contribute to discussions until all men have expressed their opinions.

Where I live in southeast England, men often address one another as 'mate' in informal situations. (*"Hey, mate, give me that knife. Cheers, mate."*) Women don't do that.

Consider the society depicted in your novel. What are the expectations of male and female behaviour? Find ways to reflect them in your dialogue.

If you're a woman, go to a place where you can eavesdrop on men (such as a diner where builders go for breakfast) and observe their speech patterns. If you're a man, do the same in a place where women often meet, such as a tea shop. Best keep a notebook and pen at hand, so you can jot down your observations.

For stories set in other cultures, you may need to ask a native to point out differences in the way women and men talk.

ASSIGNMENT

Take a dialogue scene you've drafted, if possible one where a man and a woman talk. Tweak it a little to make the male character sound more typically male or woman more female. Do this in a way that suits the individual characters and fits the story.

12. HOW TO MAKE CHARACTERS APPEAR INTELLIGENT

Readers like to read about characters who are clever, smart, cunning or wise. Dialogue is great for this.

Here are some handy tricks to make readers perceive a character as intelligent.

HOW INTELLIGENT CHARACTERS TALK

Please note that this is about fiction, and doesn't necessarily reflect how real life people behave.

1. The intelligent character's speech is focussed, tight and to the point, without filler words.
2. She asks a lot of questions. This shows an enquiring mind and perceptiveness.
3. She probably doesn't use profanity because she doesn't need swearwords to prop up her arguments, although there may be exceptions. (See Chapter 19.)
4. She understands the other person's perspective.
5. In an argument (see Chapter 25) she keeps her cool, even when the other person gets nasty, interrupts her or resorts to swearing.
6. Her dialogue often has zingers. (See Chapter 5.)

HOW EDUCATED PEOPLE TALK

Intelligent people often—though by no means always—are better educated than others. You can reflect this in their individual voices.

Writing Vivid Dialogue

1. The educated person has a richer vocabulary. Give her a wider range of words than the other characters.

2. She'll use slightly longer words. For example, when other characters use only words with one or two syllables, she uses words with one, two, three or four. But don't overdo the use of long words, or the reader will think she's conceited.

3. Her sentences are more complex. When she talks, the sentences may be a little longer and complex, with subordinate clauses. But don't make the sentences too complicated, or her speech will sound unnatural.

4. If she's the snobbish type who likes to show off her superior education, sprinkle some phrases in Latin or a foreign language into her dialogue. She may also quote Shakespeare, Aristotle and Machiavelli at every opportunity.

5. The highly-educated snob may gain pleasure from correcting other people's errors.

ASSIGNMENT

Does your work in progress have a character who is more intelligent or more educated than the others?

Tweak this character's dialogue to get this across. A few small word changes are probably enough.

13. DIALOGUE FOR MULTIPLE CHARACTERS

When several people talk, it gets confusing for the reader. You, the author, are responsible for clarity. This requires careful orchestrating.

Here are some tips. While they are not rules, I recommend that you follow them as far as is practical.

1. Use as few characters as possible.

Can you eliminate some people? If they're not needed for the scene, don't invite them.

Even if they are in the room, they don't necessarily take part in the conversation, as long as you give them a reason for their silence. The teenage daughter may sulk and refuse to talk, the nerdy guy is so engrossed in his gadget that he rarely even looks up, and the uncle is snoring in his armchair by the fireplace.

2. All characters are familiar to the reader.

Introduce all the participants earlier in the book. If your reader knows who they are, she can follow them more easily.

3. Let characters join or leave halfway through.

Not everyone needs to be present every time. Maybe John arrives late to the session, after the others have already exchanged their views, and perhaps Mary walks out in a huff before the meeting is over. You can also send a character out of the room to make a phone call or to fetch more drinks.

4. Don't share the whole conversation.

Give the reader only excerpts, the bits which are important to the story. The rest is background noise and can be ignored.

If you're telling the story from the perspective of a Point of View character, share only the parts this character is involved in.

5. Focus on two people at a time.

Try to break the group dialogue into smaller chunks, each with just two people talking. This way, it's like a series of mini dialogues. John talks first with Mary, then with Abdul, and later he continues his chat with Mary.

6. Use names.

In group conversations, you need to use names more often than you normally would, to help the reader keep track of who says what. This means more beats and more tags. The characters may also address one another by name more often, for example, *"That's interesting, John. And what do you think, Mary?"*

7. Mix male and female characters.

When several people are present, it's difficult for the reader to keep track of who 'he said' refers to. It's easier if some characters are male and some female than if everyone is a 'he'.

8. Use speech patterns.

If you have established that certain characters talk in certain ways, emphasise those patterns more than usual. This helps the reader recognise the voices. For example, one character may talk in short clipped sentences, another may gush superlatives, while a third frequently exclaims, "By Jupiter!"

For a refresher about this technique, see Chapter 6.

SAMPLE DIALOGUE FROM *STORM DANCER*

In this scene, Dahoud is the new ruler of Koskara. His rule has been imposed on the locals who resent it. He has made the controversial decision to staff his government with natives. Now he needs to persuade them to swear loyalty to his overlord.

Ten people are present, but only five of them talk – the characters the reader has already met in previous scenes. Their personalities and agendas come through in every word, although you probably won't pick up the subtleties since you're not familiar with these people yet. Another important speaking character will arrive later in the scene.

As soon as Dahoud invited the councillors to swear loyalty, arms crossed over chests.

"We're Koskarans," Wurran said. "We won't pledge obedience to the Quislaki Queen and her Consort."

Dahoud had expected the refusal. "Will you--"

"But you absolutely must!" Esha hit her stylus on the tablet. "You can't be a member of our council until you do."

"I'll take the oath, Dahoud," Keera said. "You can count on me."

"Some folks will swear any oath." Wurran's nose crinkled as if at a bad smell. "Some folks are so ambitious, they serve abusers. Some folks desert in a crisis to throw their lot in with the enemy."

Keera remained unflustered, not a single muscle twitched in her face. "In war, brave people take up arms and fight. Clever people infiltrate the enemy. Cowards do nothing and just wait until it's over."

The reddening of Wurran's cheeks revealed that the arrow had hit. "It takes a thousand years for a lizard to grow into a snake," he hissed. "And only one year for a disloyal person to grow into a traitor."

Wurran's sole known act of courage had been the refusal to trade with the Black Besieger. Did he carry the shame of cowardice? But Dahoud would not encourage rancour in his council. He sent Keera a warning glance, which she answered with a shrug.

"I don't want your oaths to Quislak," Dahoud said. "What counts is your loyalty to Koskara. Are you prepared to swear that oath?"

They remained silent. Then their heads turned to Mansour, waiting for his command.

"We will," Mansour said. "Will you?"

ASSIGNMENT

Either try your hand at writing a scene with three or more characters, applying as many of the above techniques as the plot allows.

Or revise a scene you've already written, and aim to make it easier for the reader to follow.

14. WHEN AND HOW TO USE BODY LANGUAGE

Body language is a fantastic tool for fiction authors, and I suggest you use it a lot. Body language achieves several functions in just a few words:

- It attributes the speech to the speaker, without any need for 'he said'-type tags. (See Chapter 7.)
- It can break up long speeches without disrupting the flow.
- It conveys the speaker's mood and attitude.
- It emphasises what the speaker says.
- It can contradict the speaker's words, hinting at secrets and dishonesty. (See Chapter 15.)
- It can speak even when the character keeps his mouth shut.

GESTURE, POSTURE, FACIAL EXPRESSION, TONE OF VOICE

As a writer, you can use four types of body language clues:

- gesture
- posture
- facial expression
- tone of voice

Let's look at them one by one.

Gesture

Gestures work best before the speech, or in the middle of the speech.

Examples:

She pointed to the orchard. "I saw him there."

He slammed his fist on the table. "I've had enough."

She scratched her chin. "Are you sure this will work?"

"Welcome." He pointed to the couch. "Why don't you make yourself comfortable?"

Posture

This works best before or in the middle of the speech.

Examples:

She raised her chin. "You can't make me do this."

He locked his arms across his chest. "No way."

She leant away from him. "This isn't working between us."

"I consider this an insult." He stood with his shoulders squared and his legs braced. "Take it back."

Facial Expression

This works best before or in the middle of the speech.

Examples:

Her eyes narrowed. "You expect me to believe this?"

His cheeks turned tomato-red. "What do you mean?"

"I'm sorry." She stared at the floor. "I didn't want it to be this way."

The corners of his eyes crinkled, and his lips twitched. "Really?"

Tone of Voice

This works best after or in the middle of the speech.

"We will stand together in this." His voice was deep and resonant like a church bell.

"I've told you a hundred times, and I'm telling you again." Her voice sounded like a dentist's drill, high-pitched and persistent. *"Why don't you ever listen?"*

"You know that I'm going to kill you, don't you?" He sounded as casual as if he was discussing the weather. *"Do you prefer a shot in the heart, or the head?"*

"You've been with that floozy again, you cheating bastard!" Her voice was loud enough to wake up the whole neighbourhood.

BODY LANGUAGE CLUES OVER-USED BY NOVICE WRITERS

Editors can tell if a writer is experienced or a beginner by looking at the body language in the manuscript. Submissions by novices are full of characters smiling, sighing, frowning, nodding, shrugging, biting lips, raising brows and taking deep breaths to steady themselves.

Experienced authors use a wide range of body language clues.

BODY LANGUAGE CLUES FOR DIFFERENT SITUATIONS

Here are some sentences you might use to convey body language. These are just a starting point to give you ideas. You'll need to tweak them to suit your story and your characters. You may be able to find much better ones!

Shy: *She blushed. Her cheeks fired. He shuffled his feet. She looked at the hands in her lap. She studied her sandals. He cleared his throat.*

Embarrassed: *His face turned scarlet. His face reddened like a tomato. He looked at his shoes.*

Anxious: *She gnawed at her nails. She fidgeted with her necklace. The hand holding the pint glass shook. Her fingers twisted the cup around and around.*

His hands fluttered at his collarbone. He adjusted his shirt collar and pulled at his tie.

He stood with his legs tight together and one hand locked around the other. He glanced over one shoulder, then over the other. He pulled out his wallet from the chest pocket, flipped through its contents without looking, and shoved it back. He checked his wallet, pulled at his cuffs and wound up his watch. He rubbed his hands as if soaping them under a stream of icy water.

Angry: *His fist clenched. His voice rose. His face reddened. Her lips tightened. He stared as if he wanted to kill me with his eyes. He stomped a foot on the floor. She slammed a palm on the desk.*

Aggressive: *She jabbed a finger at me. He stood so close I could smell the toothpaste on his breath.*

Dishonest: *She rubbed her nose. He leaned forward. His voice had the deep, well-rehearsed tone of a professional performer. Her eyes were wide, and blinking fast.* (More about lying characters in Chapter 15.)

Hiding a secret: *She gazed past him. She did not meet his eyes.* (More about this in Chapter 15.)

Impatient: *His feet drummed against the floor. She tapped her talons on the table. He tapped his pencil on the desk. She glanced at her watch.*

Disapproving: *He pursed his lips. Her eyes narrowed. He frowned. Her brows furrowed.*

Surprise: *Her eyes widened. His eyebrows rose.*

Frightened: *She rubbed her neck. She clasped a hand to her throat. Her eyes widened. He paled. The colour drained from his cheeks. His voice rose to a shriek. An oily film formed on her forehead. Rivulets of sweat ran down the side of her cheeks. Wet patches formed around his armpits.*

Comfortable: *He sat with his legs crossed. He laced his hands behind his head. She leant back and stretched her legs out before her.*

Contempt for others: *Her nose crinkled. She picked a piece of lint from her jacket sleeve.*

Arrogant: *His lip curled. He peered down his nose at her.*

Confident: *He steepled his hands, fingertip to fingertip. She held her chin high. He spread his arms over the backs of the neighbouring chairs. He spoke in a loud, clear voice.*

Confrontational: *She squared her shoulders and lifted her chin.*

Distressed: *He rubbed his forehead. She twisted her necklace.*

Guilty: *He turned his head to the side, avoiding her eyes.*

Insecure: *She played with her bracelet. She sat with her palms on her thighs. He shrugged. He adjusted his tie. She hooked her feet behind the legs of her chair.*

Relieved: *Her shoulders relaxed.*

Disappointed: *His head dropped.*

Amused: *The corners of his mouth twitched.*

Happy: *Her feet wiggled. Her eyes sparkled. He beamed. The corners of his eyes crinkled.*

Sad: *Tears streaked down her dusty face. The corners of her mouth drooped.*

Worried: *He massaged his shoulders. She rubbed a hand down the side of her belly. He scratched his scalp. She sat with her shoulders hunched up to her ears. She licked her lips.*

Shocked: *He stiffened. She paled.*

Stressed: *She hugged herself and rubbed her shoulders. He stroked the front of his neck. He wrung his hands. His lips narrowed until they disappeared. He pulled at his collar as if it was too tight.*

I suggest you paraphrase these examples creatively, to avoid the novice flags.

BODY LANGUAGE AND POINT OF VIEW

Most of the time, people aren't aware of their body language, although they see other people's. Don't show the Point of View character's body language, but that of the other characters he sees.

For example, if Mary is the PoV, the following sentences wouldn't work:

Mary's face turned the colour of tomato ketchup.
The corners of Mary's eyes crinkled with merriment.
A deep frown appeared on Mary's forehead.

The only kind of body language you can use for the PoV is what she's aware of. This includes deliberate gestures.

Mary pointed at the exit.
Mary dug her nails into her palms.
Mary slammed a palm on the table.
Mary hugged her arms to her chest.

With men, posture shifts are often conscious and intentional (see Chapter 14), so if the PoV is male, you can include posture clues for him as well as for the other characters.

John braced his legs and squared his shoulders.
John stepped to the side and leaned away.

USING BODY LANGUAGE TO CONTRADICT THE WORDS

Hint at dishonesty or secrets by showing body language that contradicts what the character says. This is an advanced technique and highly effective, as long as you use it sparingly.

Examples:

"No need to hurry." Mary drummed her fingers on the table.
Mary glanced at her watch. "Take all the time you need."
"I can wait," Mary assured him. Her feet jiggled and bounced.

ASSIGNMENT

Revise a dialogue scene you've written, adding several body language clues.

Now read the scene as if you were a reader who's bought this book. Can you see the body language? Great job!

15. TELLING LIES

Almost every novel has at least one scene where a character tells a lie, and several where someone doesn't tell the whole truth. The PoV and the reader may have niggling suspicions, but they don't know. This uncertainty creates suspense.

But how do you achieve this suspicion without certainty in the reader's mind?

THE BODY LANGUAGE OF LIARS

Liars often display certain body language clues, not knowing that their body reveals them:

- Lots of smiles.
- Rapidly blinking eyes.
- Frequently pursed lips.
- Head moves hardly at all.
- Arm gestures are small.
- Statements end with hand gestures.
- Leaning forward, often with elbows on knees.
- Touching the face a lot, especially mouth and nose.
- Touching neck, hands, arms.
- Avoiding the other person's eyes (inexperienced liars, ashamed of telling lies).
- Gazing firmly into the other person's eyes (experienced liars, e.g. confidence tricksters).

THE WORDS OF LIARS

Certain words, certain ways of phrasing answers, and certain tones of voice can be clues that a person is lying:

- Mispronouncing words, Freudian slips.
- A lot of 'um', 'er', 'uh'.
- During an unplanned lie, the pitch of the voice often goes up.
- During deliberate deceptions, the voice often drops.
- "Believe me", Honestly", "To be perfectly honest", "In all honesty", "To tell the truth".
- Deceivers give lengthy answers to simple questions.
- Deceivers complain a lot.

Note: liars are not the only people who do these things. Honest people do them too, sometimes, especially when they are nervous. Therefore, these body language clues aren't proof that someone is lying. They only indicate that someone **may** be lying.

The more of these clues you cluster together, the stronger the suggestion of untruth.

Examples:

"How would I know where your wallet is?" He did not meet her eyes. "I have no idea, honestly."

She fingered the pimple on her nose. "Honestly, Mum, I wasn't there. They, like, went without me."

"You must believe me!" Her voice rose to a screech. "I didn't go there. Honestly, I didn't."

"I didn't do it, officer. And I resent your allegations. You're picking on me because I'm, eh, Chinese. You always harass ethnic minorities." He slammed a palm on the table. "I will register a formal complaint about you, that's what I'll do."

He leant forward. "Trust me, Mrs Smith. Your investments will be safe. They'll double within two months." He spoke with the deep, assured voice of a well-rehearsed performer. "To tell the truth, they'll double within a week."

ASSIGNMENT

Find a scene in your fiction draft where a character tells a lie or an incomplete truth. Many short stories and almost all novels have such a situation.

Write or revise this scene so the reader gets a hint. It can be a tiny hint or a strong one, depending on how much suspicion you want to arouse in the reader at this stage.

16. STARTING A STORY WITH DIALOGUE

Some writers have declared the rule that you must never begin a novel with dialogue. Others decree that you always should. Ignore them.

If handled well, a dialogue opening pulls the reader right into the story.

HOW NOT TO DO IT

Here's an example which doesn't work:

"This is where you'll die."
"What makes you sure? Plans change."

The reader doesn't know who says what, who the people are, where this conversation takes place, from whose perspective she experiences it, and what it's all about. Her reaction is 'Huh?' Confused rather than intrigued, she may not bother to read on. Instead of clicking 'Buy Now' she'll download the next free sample.

HOW TO DO IT

Compare these three variations. Each contains the same dialogue lines, but promises a different story.

"This is where you'll die." The Arab's voice echoed through the gorge.
John strained at the rope biting into his wrists. "What makes you sure? Plans change."

In this version, the reader knows that the scene is outdoors, that one of the characters is an Arab and that John by implication is not, that John is the Arab's captive and that the scene represents John's Point of View.

Writing Vivid Dialogue

Many questions remain open—how did John get into this situation, and what will he do next?—but the reader knows enough to understand what's going on and to be curious about the rest.

> "This is where you'll die." The guard's lips tightened with compassion, and she didn't meet my eyes.
> "What makes you sure?" I scanned the bare room, the concrete floor, the high windows. "Plans change."

Here the reader knows that the guard is female, and even that she's compassionate and uncomfortable in her role. The reader experiences the story from the prisoner's perspective. The location is indoors, and there's a hint at plans of escape.

The reader knows enough to understand where she is in this story, and wants to learn more—will the narrator escape? Why is the narrator supposed to die? What's the relationship between the prisoner and the guard? How will the prisoner escape?

> I point my sabre at the gallows on the other side of the square. "This is where you'll die."
>
> Lady Mary scans the ragged crowds gathered to witness her execution and wrinkles her nose. "What makes you sure?" She shrugs a delicate shoulder. "Plans change."

In this version, the reader gets a sense of the location—a public square—and of the period—a time when people wore sabres and execution was by public hanging. The Point of View character is someone who bears arms and is thus in a position of power or authority. Mary is an aristocrat who is arrogant, snobbish and unafraid.

This is enough for the reader to get a taste of what the story is like—historical fiction, with class struggle and violence—and whether she wants to read it.

TIPS

Here are some techniques to pull off a dialogue-based opening. These are suggestions, not rules, so feel free to discard any that don't fit your story.

- Use two characters, no more, otherwise the reader feels confused and struggles to work out who is who and wants what.
- Make the dialogue about something exciting. Don't waste it on small talk.
- Don't use the first few dialogue lines to convey information. Info-dumps at the beginning of a book are a put-off. (See Chapter 17.)
- Don't use tags. 'He said, she replied' doesn't add anything of value beyond telling the gender of the speakers, and is too boring for this important part of the book.
- Use beats—any kind of action or body language.
- Include a hint about the location.
- Quickly establish which of the two characters will frame the Point of View.
- If writing in third person, give the Point of View character's name to make him real in the reader's mind.
- If possible, let the non-PoV character speak first, and the PoV react. This feels more natural than the other way round.

If this seems a lot to put into a few lines, remember that small clues are enough. You don't need to describe the setting in detail, but the reader needs to know if it's indoors or outdoors. A biography of the characters is also unnecessary as long as you give a hint about their role.

ASSIGNMENT

Think of a story you want to write. If you're like most writers, you probably have a wealth of ideas waiting to be developed. Choose one where you could start with a dialogue between two people. Write a draft.

Or

Rewrite the beginning of your current work in progress so it starts with dialogue—but only if you feel that this suits the story.

17. INFORMING WITHOUT INFO-DUMPING

Dialogue is a great way to convey information to the reader—but beware info-dumping. 'Info-dumps' are sections where the author force-feeds the reader with information, and the reader, bored, skips those paragraphs to get back to the story.

INFO-DUMPS TO AVOID

You need to keep away from two types of info-dump in your dialogue: the 'As-You-Know-Bob' and the 'Master-Tell-Me-How' devices.

1. As-You-Know-Bob

When characters tell one another things they already know, the dialogue feels unnatural. Here are two examples:

Mary faced her husband across the kitchen table. "As you know, Bob, we're short of money. We took out a mortgage on this house three years ago when your father died. Our eldest son John is attending college, and we are struggling to pay the tuition fees."

"As you know, John, this apparatus is crucial for casting the cogwheels used by the nation's fleet of dirigibles," *Mary said,* "so let me give you a quick reminder how it works. Listen carefully, because this is important."

2. Master-Tell-Me-How

To heap a lot of information on the reader at once, writers may resort to a question-and-answer device. A character (often an eager student or apprentice) asks about the background of something, or how it works, and listens attentively as the master (or teacher, grand-

Writing Vivid Dialogue

mother, guru, wise old man) imparts the knowledge. However, the readers aren't as attentive as the fictional apprentice. After two sentences, their eyes glaze over and they skip.

Here is an example:

"Master, tell me how cogwheels are made with this apparatus," the boy requested.

The master demonstrated. "First you turn this lever. Then you turn this wheel and... [insert paragraph of instructions.]"

"Thank you," the boy said eagerly. "Where do the cogwheels go when they are finished?"

The master showed him a map. "Here, at the Blue Steam river, is the dirigible factory where most of the national fleet's vessels are assembled. Ever since our Queen came to the throne... [insert info-dump about geography history and technology]."

HOW TO CONVEY INFORMATION IN DIALOGUE

Here are some techniques to try in your fiction:

* Readers need less information than you may think, so reveal only as much as is necessary for the understanding of the plot.

* As a rule of thumb, feed the readers information in morsels—a word here, a sentence there—spread over several pages.

* To make the readers aware of a difference between their reality and the story's fictional world, let characters mention the different item in passing, showing that they take it for granted.

Let's say you're writing an urban fantasy novel and want to alert your readers that werewolves exist. Weave some casual mentions of werewolves into their conversations, perhaps like this:

"Auntie, I've been to the zoo! I've seen werewolves and lions and tigers and a big grey elephant!"

On the next page, Mary chats with her friend:

"I've seen the most amazing dress, dark grey like a werewolf's pelt, with a plunging neckline and silver appliqués at the hem. I must have it."

* To arouse the readers' interest in a subject, withhold the information. The technique of avoided answers works well here. (See Chapter 2.)

"Have you ever seen a werewolf in these parts?"
"We have a lot of interesting wildlife here. I shot a wild boar once, the biggest beast ever, weighed in at nearly three hundred pounds. I had the tusks made into bracelets for my wife. Mary, show him your bracelets, will you?"

ASSIGNMENT

Think of an item of information you want to convey to your readers. Insert the clues in small subtle portions.

Or

If you've used info-dumping dialogue, revise that scene by breaking the information into several small pieces and serving them in interesting ways.

18. INTERNAL DIALOGUE: THINKING, NOT TALKING

Every rule book and style sheet insists on a different format for character thoughts: single quote marks, double quote marks, no quote marks at all, tags, no tags, past tense, present tense, speech, indirect speech, direct italics... Whichever method you choose, someone will tell you it's 'wrong'.

I'm not going to complicate matters by decreeing yet another set of rules. Simply pick one method and apply it consistently to the whole manuscript, unless a paying publisher requests otherwise.

Instead, let's look at how to make those thoughts riveting, because that's the skill that counts.

Character thoughts (also called 'introspection' or 'internal dialogue') slow down the story's pace, which is sometimes desirable but more often it's not. They are among the bits many readers skip. Don't let that happen to your story.

Here are some tips:

1. Use internal dialogue sparingly. Often, it's enough (and better) to imply the character's attitudes through his actions or visceral responses.

2. Keep the thoughts short. If a thought is short, it won't slow the pace much, and readers won't skip it. The shorter, the better.

   Instead of
   'I wonder what's the best thing for me to do in this situation now.'
   write
   'What now?'

3. Stories told in First Person (I) can have more thoughts than Third Person (he, she). Thoughts feel more natural in First Person, and they don't disrupt the plot flow, so if it suits your story, the character's thoughts can span several sentences. For First Person stories, it's probably best to render thoughts without quote marks or italics.

4. Don't use tags if you can avoid them. Thought tags (he thought, she realised, he wondered, she considered) call attention to themselves and create a barrier between the reader and the experience. However, if a scene needs thought tags for clarity, use them.

5. If you use thought tags, keep them short. As a magazine editor, I often received submissions by novice writers with sentences like this:

   "That's it,' she thought silently to herself in her head. Hmm—where else would she think but in her head? To whom else but herself? In any other way than silently? It's enough to write *'That's it,' she thought.*

6. First Person PoV and Third Person Deep PoV don't need any attribution at all. It's clear who's thinking, because the reader sees only inside that one character's mind.

Instead of
The door slammed in my face. 'What now?' I wondered.
you can simply write
The door slammed in my face. What now?

7. If you need to attribute a thought at all—for example, if the story is told in Omniscient PoV—use beats rather than tags. (I'm not adding an example here because establishing Omniscient PoV would require a lengthy excerpt.)

8. In Deep PoV stories, you can contrast what the PoV character thinks with what he does. This can be done in the same tense as the dialogue, or in the same tense as the narrative, either in Direct Speech or Indirect Speech—use whatever suits your story best.

"Will Daddy be home for Christmas?"

"He'll do what he can to be here with us." *The swine won't come if he can help it. He'll stay cosy with his new family.*

Lady Mary's lips ached from keeping the polite smile in place. "How interesting. Tell me more." *She couldn't wait to get away from the boring vulgarian.*

ASSIGNMENT

Find a section in your work in progress where a character has thoughts. Tweak it so the thoughts feel natural and don't disrupt the story flow.

Or

Write a short section where the PoV character thinks something between talking and acting. Remember to keep the thoughts short.

19. INSULTS AND PROFANITY

Do your characters cuss, curse and swear?

I'm not going to tell you that you must always or never use swearing in your fiction. That is for you to decide. However, I'm going to give you some aspects to consider, as well as techniques how to use profanity to good effect if you choose.

Please don't think that your characters have to swear 'because everyone swears on TV' or 'so they sound like real men'.

Dialogue with profanity doesn't necessarily sound more realistic than without. Nor does it have more impact.

Decades ago, swearwords in literature were so rare that if a character cussed, the readers blinked and stared. Now there's so much swearing going on in books and movies, the effect has worn off. Most of the time, the f-word has the same effect as 'really, very, kind of, dunno maybe, err'—it dilutes and weakens what is said. 'Dropping the f-bomb' doesn't create a shocking explosion, it elicits a yawn.

Consider your intended audience. In some genres—such as Inspirational Romance—swearing is taboo, in others, it depends on the publishing house. Many publishers won't accept foul language in manuscripts, and many readers won't tolerate it in books. Unless you're certain that your book will be viewed only by cuss-friendly people, it may be best to err on the side of caution.

WHEN TO USE PROFANITY

When your characters use swearwords, this has several effects, some desired, some undesired. Consider them before you decide, and remember that they don't necessarily reflect the speech patterns of real-life people.

Writing Vivid Dialogue

- Characters who use a lot of foul language come across as unintelligent. Is this an effect you want? Probably not for the hero, the villain and other important characters, although it can be useful for the villain's minion. (In real life, a person can be an astrophysicist with an IQ of 150 and swear all the time, but this is fiction, and we're looking at how readers perceive fictional characters.)

- In a discussion or confrontation, the person who uses foul language is perceived as having the weaker arguments. He comes across as needing to bolster his feeble reasoning with swearing. You can use this when two characters argue: one of them uses more and more swearwords. This signals to the reader that the cusser is losing the argument and knows it.

  Let's say two war leaders argue over who should hold a fortress. Each presents his points and argues his position, and at first they use similar language. Then:

  "In this case, you don't need the fortress and can surrender it."
  "I won't fucking surrender the fucking fortress. It's my fucking right to stay."

  Put yourself in the reader's mind. Which of the two comes across as the stronger one here?

- If a character never uses foul language, and two thirds into the book he suddenly yells a curse, the impact is great. It signals that the situation is serious.

- In some milieus where swearwords are part of everyday language—say, among the members of an inner city gang—dialogue will feel stilted if you censor the words. You don't need to insert as much profanity into those scenes as there would be in real life, but you may decide to sprinkle some token words into the dialogue.

- For 'fish out of the water' stories in which a character enters a different milieu for which his upbringing has not equipped him, the use of foul language can emphasise the different lifestyles. For example, if you place a convent-reared girl among dock workers in the harbour, the use of foul language for the men and the non-use for her will sharpen the contrast.

- Swearwords, curses and insults can serve as backstory hints and for world-building.

INVENTING SWEARWORDS, CURSES AND INSULTS

Here is how to bypass most language censors, entertain your readers, enrich your book with world-building, and have creative fun at the same time: invent new swearwords!

Words like 'damn', 'hell', 'bloody', 'fucking' are dull. Don't dilute your dialogue with them.

Instead, invent new words and phrases.

By the big barnacle, I'll keelhaul your black-spotted butt, you puking barge-rat!

Waves of weevils! Waves of weevils!

Writing Vivid Dialogue

1. Consider your characters' backgrounds. What environment do they come from? What's their job?

   Use words from that environment to form curses.

   When things go wrong, a sailor may grumble *"Barges and barnacles!"* and yell *"You scurvy-mouthed ship rat!"*

   The physicist may utter *"Crying chronon!" "By all the quarks!"* or *"You higgs-bosomed wormhole!"*

   Take care not to over-use this technique. If characters constantly use funny profanities, it creates a comedic effect.

2. If you've invented a society, allow uncouth people to use the names of the spirits and deities in a foul manner, often combined with words relating to genitals or bodily functions. This works especially well if the words alliterate (start with the same sound). Let's say the community worships the gods Tivla, Avalti and Bordok, then people may swear *"Tivla's tits!" "Avalti's arse!"* or *"Bordok's balls!"* Of course, the priests and educators of this society try to stamp out this casual blaspheming.

3. In fantasy fiction, you can use swearwords to hint at differences between that world and reality as we know it. Does the planet have three moons, is the community menaced by vampires? Let a character exclaim, *"By the three moons!"* or *"Vampire's teeth!"* and the reader gets an inkling of what's going on.

4. Look up insults from other cultures and periods, and tweak them for your story. The internet is a great resource for this. How about *"You curly-headed onion!"* from ancient Rome, or *"You turtle egg!"* from modern China?

5. When inventing curses and insults, mention body parts and bodily functions (caution—those may be too similar to modern swearwords and thus not work as creative alternatives), painful experiences and the person's ancestors: *("A curse upon your ancestors!" "May a thousand fireants crawl into your butt!")*

EXERCISE

Invent profanities to suit the following:

- A cattle rancher
- A hospital doctor
- An archaeologist
- A mountaineer
- A deep-sea diver
- A world where werewolves are a serious threat
- A world where floods are a frequent problem

ASSIGNMENT

Decide if you're going to use profanity in your writing, and if yes, how much and on what occasions. (If in doubt, do without.)

Optional: invent creative swearwords, curses and insults for the story you're working on. Have fun!

20. FOREIGN LANGUAGES, ACCENTS AND JARGON

How 'foreign' should foreigners sound? How much of their language should you render in the original? How can you make an accent heard? How do you format foreign words? How much is too much?

Before long, every writer faces this kind of question, and there are no definitive answers. However, I can show you what I've found works best in my fiction and that of other authors.

ACCENTS

If a character has a strong accent, don't write everything he says exactly as it sounds. The effect would be ridiculous.

"Wherr arr we going?" Maria asked. "I tink tis trrip is verry farr."

If you must, pick one word and show its accented pronunciation whenever the character uses it, but don't do it for every word.

A better method is to use the accent as a beat the first time this character speaks:

"Where are we going?" Maria pronounced the r's deep in her throat. "I think this trip is very far."

AMERICAN AND BRITISH ENGLISH AND OTHER VARIATIONS

American and British English use different words, and it's best if your character uses the appropriate ones.

For example, if an Englishman joins a conversation with Americans, he'll talk of 'autumn' when they say 'fall', and of 'lift' when they use 'elevator'. Don't draw attention to the differences, just use them.

Here are some words to use, first the British then the American variant:

- autumn/fall
- lift/elevator
- braces/suspenders
- suspenders/garter belt
- flat/apartment
- car park/parking lot
- crisps/chips
- chips/fries
- rubbish/garbage
- handbag/purse
- aubergine/eggplant
- courgette/zucchini
- cooker/stove
- curriculum vitae (CV)/résumé
- fish fingers/fish sticks
- colleague/co-worker
- jumper/sweater
- trousers/pants
- knickers/panties
- tights/pantyhose

These are just examples. You can find more on the internet.

Differences also exist for other regional variants of English, such as Australian or Indian English. For example, in India the word 'stitching' is used to mean 'sewing, dressmaking, tailoring'. It's best if the characters use the words common in their part of the world.

The tricky bit is whether to change the spelling as well. If your novel is in American English, and one character talks British English, you can give him British words, no problem. But should you spell everything he says in British English too? (e.g. travelled vs traveled, colour vs colour). There is no right or wrong answer here. You have to make a choice and stick with it.

Some regions have their own variants of English, often blended with remnants of an older local languages. Scots is a typical example.

To convey how a Scottish character talks, you may want to replace some English words with their Scots equivalent. Here are some Scots/English words.

- dreich/cold, wet, miserable (weather)
- wee/little
- stor/dust
- lass, lassie/girl
- bairn/child
- aye/yes
- breeks/trousers
- cloot/cloth, clothing
- crabbit/ill-tempered
- eejit/idiot
- gloaming/dusk
- paw/father
- trouchle/trouble

Please note that the words in this list are just examples for your inspiration. A full dictionary, complete with differences between Highland and Lowlands Scots and other nuances, would exceed the scope of this guide.

You'll find more on the internet. Simply sprinkle a few Scots words into the English dialogue, and don't lay it on too thick.

Apply the same principles for other regional language variants.

FOREIGN LANGUAGES

If the characters converse in a foreign language, simply write it in English. The exception is if the PoV character overhears foreigners conversing in their tongue and doesn't understand it. Then you may want to render a couple of sentences in that language—but make sure it's correct. Ask a native, don't rely on Google Translate.

However, if the conversation is in English and a foreigner struggles to communicate, you can convey this in English words with foreign sentence construction:

"I do not believe that this right is," Mary said. "My mother has this never so made."

Simply take the sentence in the original language (in this case, German) and translate it word for word, without adjusting the syntax. This will sound authentic and be close to how a foreigner really talks. If you don't know the language, ask a native speaker for help.

If the foreigner has mastered the language, use correct English grammar, but perhaps with simple word choices and sentence constructions.

Don't use foreign words when foreigners speak English. They wouldn't use them, so the dialogue would ring false. The exception is concepts which cannot be translated into English. Some phrases simply don't have an English equivalent. The foreigner, groping for a way to translate her thought, may give up and use the familiar term in her mother tongue.

Another possible exception is a habit word. For example, an Arab may say *'Inshallah'* if she's used to saying that a lot. As a German who's lived in Britain for more than twenty-five years, I speak English, write books in English, think in English, and I certainly don't use German words when talking with Britons. However, the word *'ja'* (German for 'yes', 'yeah' or 'yep') sometimes slips in.

How do you format the foreign words? The modern way is not to format them in any special way. Just write them as part of the dialogue.

Examples:

"Ja, and the performance was great."
"We'll go home tomorrow, inshallah."

This is the approach I recommend. It looks (and therefore 'sounds') natural and doesn't halt the flow.

However, it's also acceptable to italicise the foreign words—in the above examples, 'ja' and 'inshallah'. This was customary in Victorian literature, at a time when authors frequently inserted phrases (and whole poems and quotations) in Latin or French to demonstrate their erudition. These days, a writer showing off her knowledge is frowned upon, lengthy quotes are considered dull, and italicised foreign words feel disruptive. But some publishers' house styles still ask for foreign words to be italicised, and if the publisher pays you, bow to their wish.

An issue that has caused me headaches is whether to capitalise the foreign words if they're capitalised in the original language. I feel they should be, because it's part of the correct spelling, but it looks wrong in English text, so I've stopped doing that.

FANTASY LANGUAGES

Writers of science fiction and fantasy often enjoy inventing foreign languages. Then, having invested all the time and imagination, they want to show off the result of their labour. Unfortunately, this seldom works well.

The same advice applies to invented languages as to real foreign tongues: write the dialogue in English.

Use words from that fantasy language only when the English language has no equivalent.

Unless the story's plot is about linguistics, it's seldom worth inventing details of a language.

By the way, when writing science fiction, many novices create alien languages filled with apostrophes, typically with a lot of T and L: *"T'Leptl'lll,"* she said. *"L'T'llat'p'l't."* This may draw the ridicule of serious fans of the genre.

JARGON

When experts talk among themselves, they use terminology outsiders may not understand.

In many ways, this is similar to a regional variant of the English language: the syntax and most words are the same, but some words differ.

When deciding whether or not to use jargon for an expert, consider who he's talking to: in chats with people outside the field, only a few jargon words will creep in, but when he talks shop with colleagues, he'll use the terms of the trade as a matter of course.

For dialogue between experts, it's good to use some jargon, but you may want to tone it down. Readers don't mind the occasional word they don't understand, but if there are too many strange terms, their mind grows hazy and they lose interest.

ASSIGNMENT

Do you have a draft manuscript where a character hails from another country or region? Tweak his dialogue so it hints at his origins.

Or

Write a brief dialogue between an American and a Briton (or between an Englishwoman and a Scot, or whatever suits your story).

Read it aloud. Can you hear the differences? Do they sound natural and right? If not, keep tweaking the piece until it works.

21. PARANORMAL AND TELEPATHIC COMMUNICATIONS

If your character sends or receives messages which are expressed like dialogue, but without audible voice, how do you present these?

Examples:

- communication by thought transmission (telepathy)
- divine messages
- aliens making contact
- communications from the dead, perhaps through mediumship
- supernatural entities (e.g. ghosts, spirits) talking
- paranormal creatures (e.g. demons) talking in ways that can be understood but don't resemble human speech.

If you wish, you can simply format those communications like normal dialogue.

Alternatively, you can emphasise their difference, for example by using a different type font (if production technology allows it), by indenting them, by using bold, italics, double underlining, all capitals, each sentence starting with a dash, or some other differentiation.

I recommend different formatting if this form of communication plays a major role in the plot. For example, in a novel about telepathy it's worth bolding or italicising all telepathic content.

You can also use 'speech patterns' to characterise this form of dialogue. Perhaps the entity speaks consistently in three-word sentences and single-syllabic words:

"Watch her hands. She speaks lies. Touch her face."

Or maybe the communication is entirely in nouns and verbs, or whatever pattern feels right for your story. Be creative.

If possible, use beats to describe the PoV's physical experience of sending or receiving the communication.

Examples:

Mary raised the crown of her head, aligned her spine and spiralled her mind into tight focus to send her message. "Where are you?"

The back of John's neck tingled, and a hot wave swept over his skin. "Where are you?" Mary's message reverberated through his skull.

SAMPLE DIALOGUE FROM *STORM DANCER*

In *Storm Dancer*, Dahoud is possessed by a djinn (demon) that drives him to commit evil deeds. Dahoud fights to resist, but the djinn is manipulative with its messages. I gave the djinn a speech pattern—everything phrased as questions—and I rendered his dialogue in italics.

Here's an excerpt. Unlike other examples in this guide, I haven't put this in all italics, so you can see how I've italicised the djinn's speech:

The djinn slithered inside Dahoud, stirring a stream of fury, whipping his blood into a hot storm. *Would she dare to disregard the Black Besieger? What lesson would he teach to punish her insolence?*

ASSIGNMENT

Does your work in progress include paranormal, alien, telepathic or otherwise 'weird' communications? Decide how to format it, and choose a fitting speech pattern.

Revise the dialogue throughout the manuscript to make it consistent.

If you don't write this kind of fiction, skip this assignment.

22. HOW CHILDREN AND TEENAGERS TALK

The youngsters in your fiction should talk differently from the grown-ups. For authentic dialogue, let them talk like real kids of their age group.

> Mom, can I please have some orange juice?

> Mom, get me an OJ. I'm dying of thirst.

Small children have a limited vocabulary of mostly short words. As they mature, they use a wider repertoire of words.. if they want to.

For parents, it's easy to get the tone right, but if you don't have kids yourself, this can be difficult.

I've asked parents to 'translate' some sentences into kidspeak.

Writing Vivid Dialogue

"MOTHER, MAY I HAVE SOME ORANGE JUICE?"

Age 2: *"Juice, Mama?"*

Age 3-5: *"Juice please, Mommy."*

Age 5: *"Momma, I want orange juice."*

Age 5: *"Mommy, I want juice."* (Followed by reminder to say 'please' and brief wrangling over another lesson in basic courtesy.)

Age 5-9: *"Can I have juice?"*

Age 6: *"Mom, OJ now. Thirsty."*

Age 10: Sweetly, wheedling, accompanied by a hug. *"Mom, can I please have some orange juice?"*

Age 12: Antagonistic attitude and voice. *"Mom, can I have some orange juice?"*

Age 10-13: *"Mom, if you are up, get me a glass of orange juice."*

Age 13: *"Don't we have any juice?"*

Age 14: *"Mom, where's the juice?"*

Girl age 15: (ironic tone) *"Mom, if you are in the kitchen, can I have a glass of orange juice, pretty please with sugar on it?"*

Boy age 14-15: Dramatic entrance clasping throat. *"I'm sooo thirsty and gonna die if I don't get OJ."*

Boy age 15: *"Mom, I'm dying here. I need a glass of orange juice and I'm in the middle of my game."*

"I HAVE NO IDEA WHO ATE THAT CAKE. IT WASN'T ME."

Age 5: *"I didn't eat the cake! Did you eat the cake, Daddy?"*

Age 5-8: *"I didn't do it, Mommy, honest I didn't. The cake just disappeared."*

Age 7: *Quick shake of the head, loud voice.* "No! It was [insert name of sibling or pet]."

Age 5-9: "*I was hungry.*" or "*[Insert name of sibling or pet] probably ate it.*"

Age 10: *Wheedling tone.* "*It wasn't me, really, well maybe.*"

Age 12: *Averted eyes, slight panic.* "*I didn't do it.*"

Girl age 13-15: "*Don't look at me, I'm on a diet. I didn't touch your cake.*"

Boy age 12-15: "*So if I did eat the cake, and I'm not saying I did, how much trouble would I be in?*"

Age 14: "*There was cake?*"

Boy age 14-15: "*Um, maybe.*" *Makes quick exit out of the kitchen.*

"THIS JACKET IS UGLY. YOU CAN'T MAKE ME WEAR IT."

Age 3-5: *Folded arms.* "*It's too tight, Mommy.*" or "*It makes my arms hurt, Mommy.*"

Age 5: *(in tones of long-suffering)* "*I don't want that coat. I guess I won't wear a coat.*"

Age 5-9: "*It's ugly and my friends will make fun of me.*"

Age 5-10: "*No, I hate it, I hate it. I won't wear it ever.*"

Age 6: *Flips the arms, the hood or the sides and looks at them, finally tears the thing off with a loud "No!"*

Age 10: "*I do not like the looks of this, please don't make me wear it.*"

Age 10-17: "*It's hideous. If you like it so much, you wear it.*"

Age 12-15: "*Don't even think about it, no way am I wearing that thing.*"

Girl age 12-15: *"You're kidding, aren't you? Really, you are kidding me. No way."*

Age 14: *"It's fine. I'm not cold."*

Girl age 14: *"This is so not it. No way."*

Girl age 16-17: *"Like in public? It'd be social suicide to wear that thing."*

"THE PARTY WAS WONDERFUL. GREAT MUSIC, FANTASTIC FOOD. I HAD A GOOD TIME."

Age 3-5: "I don't want to go home."

Age 5: "The party was fun. I ate cake and candy and I played games and Lucy cried."

Age 10: "Boy, it was great. We had cake and stuff. Billy picked his nose and ate a bogger and we laughed until we peed our pants."

Age 12: "I had a good time, it was great I guess?"

Age 11-17: "It was rad. DJ rocked. Can we get pizza from [insert name]?"

Age 14: "It was fine."

Age 14: "Eh, it was okay. The cool kids were more worried about using their lint rollers and the most of the girls just pointed at everyone talking about their clothes, hair, stupid stuff like that. Oh! I saw this video on YouTube where this........" (followed by a long talk about something that has no bearing on the question.)

Teenager any age, in reply to a parent's question: "Great." or "Good." or "Fun." No details provided.

These examples are meant as a starting point. The youngsters in your story may talk differently, depending on their personality and attitudes, so tweak the speech patterns to fit.

If you write a lot about teenagers—especially in the Young Adult (YA) genre—spend time listening to or chatting with teens, to get a feel for when and how they talk.

ASSIGNMENT

1. Go somewhere where you can eavesdrop on teenage conversations—a diner or coffee shop, perhaps, the skateboard rink or a hangout in the park. Without appearing to listen, jot down some of their utterances into a notebook.

2. If you have a child or teenage character in the story you're currently working on, write or revise a section of their dialogue so it's typical for someone of their age.

23. HOW PEOPLE TALK IN HISTORICAL FICTION

The main question historical fiction authors face is how 'historical' the dialogue should sound.

If the characters talk in modern English, it feels inauthentic, but if they speak like they did in their time, the reader won't understand it.

As with many dialogue issues, the solution lies in creating an illusion of reality rather than an imitation of it.

Since your characters represent the real people of their era, they talk the language that's modern for their time... and that's best represented by modern English.

So go ahead and write the dialogue in modern English. However, I advise some modifications.

Very modern jargon feels jarring, so I suggest avoiding words which entered our vocabulary in the past fifty years such as 'down-sizing' and 'micro-managing'.

To create a period feel, sprinkle a few period terms into the text. Here are a few suggestions. Some of the words are still used in modern English, albeit less often.

VICTORIAN ENGLISH

- troth = a solemn pledge of fidelity
- cloven = split, divided
- encumbrance = burdensome obstacle
- orb = ball, sphere
- slattern = a dirty, untidy person (used as an insult)
- out-of-doors = outdoors

- to knap = to steal
- whilst = while
- mad as hops = excitable
- ticker = watch
- part-rats = half drunk
- gargler = throat
- bricky = brave, fearless
- butter upon bacon = wasteful extravagance
- chink = money (lower class slang)
- chavvy = child (lower class slang)
- flat = a person who is easily deceived (criminal slang)
- nibbed = arrested

REGENCY ENGLISH

- a trifle disguised = slightly drunk
- chit = a teenage girl
- to ding = to throw or throw away
- cut up my peace = disturb me
- a bit of muslin = a woman of easy virtue
- doing it a touch too brown = overdoing it
- cleaned out = out of money
- to flash = to show or expose something
- cutting shams = telling lies
- leech = doctor
- to toddle = to walk away slowly

- mill = fight, brawl
- too smoky by half = highly suspicious
- nabob = a rich man, especially one who made his fortune in the colonies

RENAISSANCE ENGLISH

- durst = to dare to
- fullsome = rich, plentiful
- betwixt = between
- beseech = request, beg
- dearth = scarcity, lack of
- nary = none, absolutely nothing
- nought = nothing
- to wax = to grow
- yore = years ago
- privy = toilet
- cursitor = wanderer, vagabond
- flux = dysentery
- forsooth = a mild 'oath' meaning 'I swear', suitable for casual context, polite society, women and childen.
- mint = gold

These are just examples, not intended as an exhaustive list, and they don't take into account regional variations and other nuances. Use them for inspiration and as a starting point.

If you write a lot in a specific period, it's worth researching the vocabulary of the era.

You can find glossaries on the internet, and they're free, but be careful: many period word lists focus on underworld slang which isn't how respectable nobles talked.

When using period cant, take care not to overdo it. A few words here and there are enough. Seasoned historical fiction fans will recognise them, and other readers can guess them from the context.

AUTHENTICITY VERSUS POLITICAL CORRECTNESS

People of the past didn't conform to 21st century concepts of political correctness. This causes a dilemma for authors: if the authentic language of the period contains words which are now considered offensive, should you use them or not?

The matter becomes delicate in matters of racism. For example, you would not use the word 'nigger'—but a character in the 19th century would. A plantation owner would talk about his 'nigger slaves' not his 'Afro-American staff'.

Think about how you want to handle this. I would opt for authenticity over political correctness, but you may decide differently.

You may want to aim for a compromise: the 'bad guys' use racist slurs, but the 'good guys' use words which are acceptable to modern sensitivities.

TAG STRUCTURE

To evoke a strong historical feel, especially in Renaissance and mediaeval contexts, some authors put the subject after the verb in dialogue tags.

Examples:

"Has the queen joined the hunt?" asked John.

"He'll hang for this," said Mary.

This is permissible, but feels awkward to many contemporary readers. Most prefer the modern version:

"Has the queen joined the hunt?" John asked.

"He'll hang for this," Mary said.

ALSO CONSIDER

In a historical context, there is probably a sharper distinction between the voices of educated and uneducated people (see Chapter 12) and also between people of different ranks (see Chapter 25).

SAMPLE DIALOGUE FROM *THE BLACK BOAR*

Here's an excerpt from a short fantasy horror story set in the Middle Ages.

I gave sprinkled some hints of historical words into the dialogue, especially near the beginning of the story, to create a medieval flavour, but otherwise used modern English.

I took the jug from him and filled my own mug, searching for a topic that would capture Adelida's attention. "I had the most fearsome dream last night."

"Oh, do tell, Sir Hans!" *Adelida exclaimed.* "I love dreams, most especially the fearsome ones. Indeed, I have made a study of their meanings."

I took a gulp of mead. "I dreamt I encountered a big beast of a boar, and it killed me."

Shuddering with delicate pleasure, Adelida leant forward. "What an exciting adventure! Pray, Sir Hans, tell us more. Where did it happen, and what did the beast look look like, what did it do?"

"I did not see the place, only the charging beast, for one eternal moment. It came charging it me with tusks as fat as arms, and a body as high as my waist – and I am no small man."

"Indeed not." Adelida's gaze glided over my person. Playing with her flaxen braids, she declared the dream a sign from heaven, a prophecy of a future encounter. "A boar will charge you, but forewarned by the dream, you will be prepared. Sir Bertram can advise you the best way to kill such a beast."

My rival plumped himself up like fat partridge. "Indeed. The way to get the boar is with a strong spear that won't break on impact. Easy. Just get him to charge you and aim at the throat, then it will impale itself. You just have to keep the tusks from gouging you. It's more difficult with a sword, though of course I have killed many a boar with no other weapon." He basked in the lady's admiration. She hung on his every word as he elaborated on his adventures.

I, however, could barely bring myself to listen. All the time, the vision of the furious beast remained vivid before my eyes, and I could barely eat my meat.

"Hacking at the shoulder is of no use," Bertram told me, obviously enjoying my discomfort. "An old boar's cartilage there is so thick you couldn't split it with an axe. The belly is better. The trick is to reach it without getting overrun and trampled to death."

"Hm," I said. "Uhm. Thank you."

"It's the lower tusks you have to beware. They'll rip your leg open and disembowel you."

ASSIGNMENT

If you write historical fiction, write or rewrite a section of dialogue. Aim to make it sound authentic and real, without totally imitating reality.

24. LEADERS AND FOLLOWERS, BOSSES AND MINIONS, RIVAL ALPHAS

When characters of different rank talk, the dialogue reflects their status.

Think of these examples:

- master/apprentice
- lord/serf
- parent/child
- husband/wife (in societies where women are subservient)
- lady/servant
- boss/employee
- king/subject
- knight/squire
- bishop/priest
- abbess/nun
- officer/grunt

How sharp the differences are depends on the society your story depicts. In a modern near-egalitarian world, they may be subtle, but in a historical setting they can be drastic. Either way, the role affects how people communicate.

WHO ASKS THE QUESTIONS?

The superior person is the one who asks questions, and he asks because he has the right to demand answers. His questions may be gentle, compassionate, harsh, threatening, offensive, sarcastic, about job-related matters or private issues. Without causing offence, he can ask questions like:

"*Where were you last night?*"
"*How's your wife?*"

and his subordinate, whether he likes the question or not, will answer.

The one thing the superior never asks is permission.

The person of lower rank, however, would not presume to ask questions of his boss! If he needs to ask something in the course of his duties, he'll begin with an apology. "*Excuse me, sir. Shall I show Mr John into the morning room?*"

He may ask permission. "*Sir, might I please visit my family?*"

But he will not ask questions which demand answers or intrude into the private sphere, like,

"*Where were you last night?*" or "*How's your wife?*"

COMMANDS

Superiors can and do issue commands.

These may be phrased as orders: "*Close the window!*"

They can also be phrased courteously: "*Close the window, please.*"

Or as a question: "*Would you mind closing the window?*"

They are still commands, and the subordinate won't say "*Yes, I would mind.*" But they portray the boss as a courteous, considerate person. That's useful for characterising important figures in your novel.

HIERARCHY

A character's role and dialogue can vary depending on whom he talks to. For instance, a sergeant barks orders at the grunts, but obeys the major. A clan chief expects subservience from his serfs but kneels before his king. The way he speaks changes according to the situation.

THE DIFFERENCE BETWEEN BOSSES AND LEADERS

A boss-type has inherited his rank or been appointed to it, and people obey him because they have to.

A leader has won his position by gaining his followers' respect and trust. They follow him because they like him, and because they feel his leadership is good for them.

A boss without leadership qualities can be demanding, inconsiderate, arrogant. He snaps orders and metes out punishment, and doesn't see his subordinates as human beings.

A leader treats his subordinates with consideration—phrasing his orders with courtesy, asking questions which show that he cares, motivating his followers rather than bullying them, showing appreciation, praising good work. A brief dialogue exchange between the leader and a subordinate—maybe tacked into another scene—reveals this easily.

Here's an exchange between a 'boss' type and a subordinate:

"John, bring me the ABC file, and pronto!"
"Yes, sir."
"Hurry up. And stop that stupid limp."
"Here you are, sir."
"Get back to your duties, and if Project D still isn't finished by midnight, I'll cancel your leave."
"Yes, sir."

Here's a 'leader' type in the same situation:

"John, would you bring me the ABC file, please?"
"Yes, sir."
"Thank you. Is that knee still troubling you?"
"Only in cold weather, sir."

"How's Project D going? You've done a first rate job organising it. We need it soon, or the competition will wipe us out. Do you think you can finish it today?"

"I will do my utmost, sir, even if I have to stay through the night."

"Thank you, John, I appreciate it."

In a crisis, people may desert a boss, but they'll rally around a leader.

A boss can also be a leader—for example, he may have inherited his dukedom or been promoted to sergeant, and have the love and loyalty of the people under him. This type is popular in fiction, especially for the male lead in the Romance genre. Other characters are either bosses (the cruel lord of the manor, the bullying sergeant) or leaders (the lowly gladiator leading the slave revolt).

ALPHA CHARACTERS

'Alphas' are characters with both power and natural leadership skills. They have become popular in fiction, especially as protagonists and as male leads in Romance. Their role is modelled on pack leaders in the animal world, such as wolves (male alphas) and hyenas (female alphas). It may be in part predetermined (being the eldest male of a bloodline) but above all, it is won and needs to be defended against other claimants.

In dialogue, alpha characters probably will...

- Ask questions and demand answers.
- Give orders.
- Remind others of their alpha status should anyone forget it.
- Use body language (especially posture) which claims more space than other people's.
- Talk about issues concerning territory.
- Challenge other alphas.
- Interrupt others (but they won't do this often).

ALPHA VERSUS ALPHA

When your story pitches two alpha characters against each other, sparks fly. Each claims the leadership role and expects the other to obey. This may be the most exciting dialogue in your whole book. Set this dialogue against a wild, dangerous background—a bush fire, a jungle, the peak of Mount Everest—and make it urgent that they reach an agreement. Don't waste this verbal match in a tame restaurant or boardroom setting.

SAMPLE DIALOGUE BETWEEN BOSS AND SERVANT

This excerpt is from my short story *The Holed Stone,* set in the year 1900.

In the evening, Milady rang for Emma and informed her gravely that the lady's maid had been caught at mixed sea-bathing.

Emma's jaw dropped, and her heart hammered in her throat. Had she been seen, too?

"Such scandalous behaviour is unacceptable. She will not be returning to us." Milady's voice softened. "How long have you been with us, Emma? Two years? You're good worker. Despite your youth, you would never do something improper or against the law, would you?"

"No, Milady." Emma kept eyes lowered. The carpet's green pattern swirled like water.

"Then I offer you the position of lady's maid, starting today."

"Thank you, Milady," Emma croaked as she sank into a deep curtsey.

In the corridor, she clutched the wall to steady herself against the dizzying reality. The holed stone, now dangling on a thong under her dress, had fulfilled her wish. Her future shone as bright as the summer sun, as long as Milady did not find out about this afternoon.

SAMPLE DIALOGUE BETWEEN TWO ALPHAS

This excerpt is again from *Storm Dancer.*

Dahoud is the Lord of Koskara, appointed by the ruler of the conquering nation. Mansour is Lord of Koskara, chosen and worshipped by the local population. When disaster strikes—the town collapses into a sinkhole—Dahoud naturally takes charge. So does Mansour.

The town was beyond saving, but if they acted fast, they could get out some of the survivors. Rescuers would have to contend with darkness, unstable surfaces, sinking debris, choking dust, lack of gear, the risk of drowning, and the threat of more of the mountain crashing down.

Dahoud needed ropes, spades, torches, and he needed them fast.

From the yurt site, where the earth had not cracked, people came stumbling. Their low whispers shrieked of despair. "My nieces! My nieces are in there."—"Punishment from the gods."—"Where's my mother's house? I can't see my mother's house."

Dahoud took charge, directing their panic into action. "You, you, and you. Get ropes. You two, torches. You over there, blankets and tools. Shovels, cleavers, spades. Hurry." *Some rushed to do as told, others stared with hostility. To them, he was the enemy, the usurper sent by Quislak. He scanned the growing crowd for competent lieutenants whom the Koskarans would trust.*

[...]

"Away from the edge, everyone," *Mansour's voice bellowed in the darkness.*

Here was the perfect lieutenant to whom the Koskarans would listen. "Mansour, I need you to organise supplies. Tell these people to bring ropes, torches, tools."

The rebel leader stood with his elbows spread. "Get out of the way."

"I know what I'm doing," *Dahoud assured him.*

"*Out of the way!*"

The sinkhole gurgled and slurped.

"*Mother of Mares!*" *Dahoud shouted.* "*We don't have time for this. People are trapped, the ruins are sinking, the mountain is about to collapse. Why can't you just do as I tell you?*"

Mansour shone a torch over the abyss. "*I'm Lord of Koskara. We Koskarans take care of our own.*"

With the voice which had made legions obey, Dahoud barked: "*Get the supplies! Get helpers! Get everyone else away from here!*"

The mountain rumbled, and another section of rock crashed into the void. Screams ripped the silence.

Rather than wasting precious moments arguing over leadership, Dahoud gave in. "*What do you want me to do?*"

ASSIGNMENT

Find a scene in a draft you've written where two characters of different ranks interact. Revise it so the dialogue reflects their relative ranks.

Or

Write a dialogue scene between a superior and a subordinate.

Or

Write a confrontation between two alpha characters jostling for power.

25. ARGUMENTS

When your characters argue—especially when they feel passionate about the topic—you can have a great dialogue scene.

Here are some tips to pull it off:

- Keep the argument short—shorter than it would be in real life.
- Unlike in real life arguments, the characters don't repeat every point over and over. Allow them to say everything succinctly once. You may decide to let a character make a point three times, but in this case, let the other person counter with different replies.
- Keep the sentences shorter and tighter than in real life arguments.
- Characters may interrupt one another:

    "But your mother has—"
    "Leave my mother out of this!"

- If using tags, choose verbs which convey the tone of voice: she snapped, he roared, she spat, he yelled.
- Use the body language of anger: clenched fists and jaws, stomping, slamming hands onto tables, banging doors. These make great beats. For ideas see Chapter 14. The speakers may also grab, clutch, squeeze (and possibly smash or throw) items including furniture, which is useful for placing the conversation in a location to avoid 'white space'.
- You can describe the sound of a speaker's voice as a beat to attribute the words:

    Her voice rose to a screech
    His voice slashed like a sharpened scimitar.

- Consider each character's place in the hierarchy. If one outranks the other, he will remind his opponent sharply of this. The lower-ranking person will be cautious not to cause offence—unless he is ready to challenge the other's authority. If both are of equal or similar rank, their place in the hierarchy may become part of the argument.

- If the argument about something that went wrong, one of the characters may say 'I told you so':

    "How many times did I warn you that the wall would crack under pressure? But did you listen?"

- If they trade insults, consider using creative ones. (See Chapter 19.)

ASSIGNMENT:

Does your current work in progress contain an argument scene? Write or revise it, using body language and tone of voice.

26. FLIRTATIOUS BANTER

FLIRTATIOUS BANTER

When two characters discover their attraction for each other, but aren't ready yet to admit it to themselves and still unsure of the other's inclinations, they test the ground with flirtatious dialogue.

At first, everything they say has an innocuous meaning as well as a teasing one, so if their overture gets rejected, they can pretend it never happened.

Gradually, one of them gets bolder than the other, revealing the attraction a witty way which allows the other to either notice or ignore it. Here's an example, provided by author Alice Gaines:

Mary stared out over the ocean. "What a beautiful view."
"It certainly is."
"But, you're not looking at the ocean."
He gazed into her eyes. "There's an ocean nearby?"

This takes courage… but if rebuffed, he can still pretend that he was joking.

OPENING GAMBIT: TALK ABOUT CLOTHES

Any comment on the other person's looks or apparel – whether it's complimentary or not – signals a personal, physical interest.

Example:

Teenagers Mary and John have grown up together, and never been anything but buddies. When John says, *"You look like a sack of potatoes in this dress,"* it doesn't seem like an overture to flirtation – but it reveals that he's aware of her body for the first time. Things may develop from there.

Writing Vivid Dialogue

A man's compliments on a woman's appearance is a 'safe' flirtation opener.

Example:

When John says *"You look great. That's some dress you're wearing tonight,"* it can be read either as a statement of his attraction, or as a simple courtesy.

It's now up to Mary to decide how she interprets it. She can simply say, *"Thanks. Shall we go?"* and the matter rests. Or she can say something that keeps his attention on her appearance. *"Thanks. It's the first time I'm wearing this dress. I like the way the skirt spins when I turn – look."*

This is an invitation for him to admire the dress ... and the body inside it.

He can now switch to open flirtation – still cautious, of course – by saying something to connect the dress with himself: *"Are you wearing this for me?"* or *"How did you know blue is my favourite colour?"*

If a woman opens the flirtation by talking about the man's garments, this conveys confidence. As well as showing that she is interested in him, it signals something else: if things develop between the two, she expects to take an equal or dominant role. This works well when you write about a strong female character, and also in erotic fiction for sub/Dom scenarios.

Men rarely comment on another man's appearance. This makes compliments about clothes a useful opening gambit for gay flirtation.

"Great shirt, man," can mean *"I'm gay. Are you?"* It's discreet, without admitting anything.

If the other man is straight, he'll say so in the next sentence to discourage any advances. *"My girlfriend likes it."*

If the other man is gay and interested, he'll talk about the shirt: *"I bought it at Smithinklines. I get most of my shirts from them. You ever shop there?"*

MAKING THE FLIRTATION EXCITING

The thrill of flirtatious dialogue stems from uncertainty. Neither character knows if the other is interested, or whether their advances are welcome. They will phrase everything so it can be interpreted in two ways – either as an innocuous joke or courtesy, or as personal interest and invitation to get better acquainted.

With each exchange, the probing becomes more daring.

FLIRTATION DURING A VERBAL FIGHT

When characters argue about something, but are secretly attracted to each other, you can make the sparks fly. Readers love this. Especially in romance fiction, these are often the readers' favourite scenes.

Consult the chapter on arguments 25.

To make this dialogue sizzle with undercurrents, show that each character understands the other really well – better than she understands herself. This creates a sense of connection. You can achieve this effect even if the characters don't know one another well or meeting for the first time. Show that the 'opponent' understands the situation and emphasises, even if he doesn't budge from his own position.

Let both characters conduct the conflict with utmost fairness and honour. No nasty snide remarks, no underhanded attacks. Think of it as a sporting match where the opponents respect each other and fight fairly. Write it as a verbal sparring match.

CREATING EROTIC TENSION

In dialogue, you can create erotic tension without spelling out any sexual matters.

The technique I introduced earlier – talking about a garment – can work well. If John and Mary talk about the dress she's wearing, the reader senses that they're aware of the body inside the dress.

Talk about perfume is even more powerful, because it suggests physical proximity and heightened awareness.

"Nice cologne. Hmm... sandalwood and cinnamon?"

If you like you can then turn up the erotic tension by letting them talk about the perfume.

"I bought it in a Moroccan bazaar." Mary smiled at the memory. "The crone who sold it to me suggested I wear a few drops in my navel."

"And... did you take her advice?"

There are several ways how you can develop the dialogue from there, depending on how high you wish to ratchet up the erotic tension. Try to phrase most of the dialogue as questions. (See Chapter 1.)

You can also hint at a characters' sexual interest without mentioning sexual matters at all. Here's another example provided by erotic romance author Alice Gaines:

Mary yawned.
"Late night?" he asked.
"Coffee, please."
"Who's the lucky guy?"
She stared at him. "William Shakespeare."
"When he needs a substitute, let me know."

KEEP IT TIGHT AND USE ZINGERS

In real life, the cautious probing nature of a flirtation means that people talk in vague, often awkward ways. Hours later, they replay the dialogue in their minds and realise all the witty things they should have said.

In fiction, you can leave out the vague and awkward mumblings, and let your characters speak with sparkling wit.

A little awkwardness in a flirtation scene can be endearing if it suits the character and the situation, but don't lay it too thick.

As far as possible, let the characters talk in sizzling one-liners ('zingers' – see Chapter 5). Simply rewrite and polish every sentence until sparkles like a brilliantly cut diamond. It's worth it: your readers will adore the scene, read it over and over, and tell their friends.

ASSIGNMENT

Do you have flirtation scene in your work in progress? Revise it to make it sparkle.

Or:

Write the beginning of a flirtation between two characters who are just becoming aware of their attraction and testing the ground.

27. CREATE DRAMATIC IMPACT WITH THREESOMES AND BACK-LOADING

In this final chapter, I want to share two rhetoric devices you may want to try in your dialogue.

BACKLOADING

Whenever a character speaks, the last word has the strongest impact. Arrange the words so that a dramatic one comes at the end - something like love, death, hope, kill, truth, lies, peace.

Instead of

"Enjoy yourselves now, because you'll die tomorrow."

Write

"Enjoy yourselves now, because tomorrow you'll die."

Instead of

"I would tell you the truth if I knew it."

write

"If I knew it, I would tell you the truth."

THREESOMES

Lists of three items create drama, excitement and emotion. Yet they sound perfectly natural.

They work especially well when a character

- demands something
- needs something
- talks about upsetting events
- accuses someone
- complains
- rouses the masses
- incites violence
- infects others with fanaticism
- appeals to listeners' morals or emotions
- begs for understanding
- stirs up trouble

Examples:

"We need blankets, food and water."

"They all were there – Joe, David and Myra."

"Did you hear what gifts they brought for the baby? Gold, frankincense, and myrrh."

"Her garden overflows with flowers: dahlias, roses and marigolds."

"They worship idols! They dance naked around stone altars! They sacrifice newborn babes!"

"They smashed the windows, stole the money and poisoned the cats."

"There's only one prophet. There's only one faith. There's only one god."

"Niggers are are dirty, subhuman, evil. Find them, catch them, hang them!"

"I've cooked your favourites: spaghetti, fries and apple pie."

"I loved you, worshipped you, gave you everything you wanted, so how can you leave me?"

You can use three separate sentences for the three items, or put all three into a single sentence. You can link them with commas, or with 'and' or with 'or', or in any other way that creates a good rhythm.

Arrange the three items so the most important (or most shocking) item comes last.

Example:

"Everyone's doing it, the priests, the bishops, even the Pope."

Consider repeating a word three times in a list of three. This can add emphasis and drama.

Examples:

"Get shelter. Get an army. Get the priests to pray for us all."

"I demand justice. I demand support. Above all, I demand revenge!"

"I want to wear jeans. I want to go dancing. I want to be like a normal girl."

ASSIGNMENT

Take a dialogue scene you've written and backload several sentences. Rephrase one sentence so it becomes a list of three.

DEAR READER,

I hope you enjoyed this book and have gained many practical ideas how to refine prose.

I'd love it if you could post a review on Amazon or some other book site where you have an account and posting privileges. Maybe you can mention what kind of fiction you write, and which of the techniques suggested in this guide work best for your stories.

Email me the link to your review, and I'll send you a free review copy (ebook) of one of my other Writer's Craft books. Let me know which one you would like: *Writing Fight Scenes, Writing Scary Scenes, The Word-Loss Diet, Writing About Magic, Writing About Villains, Writing Dark Stories, Euphonics For Writers, Writing Short Stories to Promote Your Novels, Twitter for Writers, Why Does My Book Not Sell? 20 Simple Fixes, Writing Vivid Settings, How To Train Your Cat To Promote Your Book, Writing Deep Point of View, Getting Book Reviews, Novel Revision Prompts.*

My email is raynehall00000@gmail.com. Also drop me a line if you've spotted any typos which have escaped the proofreader's eagle eyes, want to give me private feedback or have questions.

You can also contact me on Twitter: https://twitter.com/RayneHall. Tweet me that you've read this book, and I'll probably follow you back.

If you find this book helpful, it would be great if you could spread the word about it. Maybe you know other writers who would benefit.

At the end of this book, you'll find an excerpt from another Writer's Craft Guide, *Writing Fight Scenes*. I hope you enjoy it.

With best wishes for your writing and successful author readings. Wow the audiences with your work!

Rayne Hall

ACKNOWLEDGEMENTS

Sincere thanks members of the Professional Authors group and my Twitter followers who critiqued the chapters, and also to the beta-readers who checked the entire manuscript before publication: Graham Downs, Ant Ryan, John Brown, Crystal Holdefer, Georgiana Kotarski and El Edwards.

The cover design for this book and others in the Writer's Craft series is by Erica Syverson. The cartoon illustrations are by Hanna-Riikka. The proofreader is Julia Gibbs.

Printed in Great Britain
by Amazon